STEPS OUT

15
STEPS OUT

by
Bob Mumford

A Study of Subjective Christianity
A Testimony of a Spiritual Itinerary

Logos International
Plainfield, New Jersey

iv

Acknowledgments

I want to thank Jorunn Ricketts for her able work in transcribing. My wife Judy for the inspirational factor and help-mate. My publisher Dan Malachuk and his wife Viola for performing "beyond the call of duty."

Preface

A man once said to me, "God hides Himself." I answered him, "Yes, that's His nature." Later that night, our conversation came back to me and I thought of John 14:21, where it says: "He that hath my commandments and keepeth them, he it is that loveth me: and he that loveth me shall be loved of my Father, and I will love him and will *manifest myself* to him."

God wants to manifest Himself to us. The Greek word for manifest means to *show plainly*. God wants to show Himself plainly to us.

How can we be sure of that? Because He has put a hunger inside us, a hunger to know more of Him. And we can be absolutely certain that God never teases. He will satisfy that hunger.

The two conditions God shows us in John 14:21 are that we *have* His commandments and that we *keep* His commandments.

Our need for God is great. The situation in the world is desperate and we need answers. We don't need anyone to point out our needs; we need answers.

God has a practical, applicable answer to

every one of our needs.

But before we can understand His answers, before He can manifest Himself to us, we must be brought out of a state of confusion into oneness with Him.

When I talk about confusion I do not mean the confusion of the world. There is compounded confusion also among God's people. Confusion comes especially when God begins to do new things in our lives.

Understanding this can bring a great release and a new sense of freedom. Although I was saved and filled with the Holy Spirit, there remained much confusion in my heart. I didn't understand what God was trying to do in my life. Psalms 120 through 134 are called Songs of Degrees. The Hebrew word for degrees is *ascent.*

These songs were probably chanted by the children of Israel as they came out of captivity in Babylon and journeyed towards Zion, the city of God. The fifteen Psalms describe fifteen lessons or principles we must learn as we move from a state of confusion into oneness with God.

The word Babylon means confusion. People often quote the text, "Come out of her (Babylon), my people, and partake not of her sins lest ye receive of her judgment." One day I began to ask myself this question, "Is coming out of Babylon geographical, or is it a spiritual experience?"

Is coming out of Babylon or religious confusion a physical deliverance? Or is coming out of Babylon an experience whereby God delivers us from the confusion in our own hearts so that we can truly understand God's will and purpose?

And I began to see that it does not really matter where you have fellowship or with whom. What matters is whether or not you have been brought out of confusion into spiritual understanding.

Coming out of confusion is God's purpose for every believer. His desire is that none *stays captive.*

One thing that has bothered me in Christendom is the tremendous escape mechanisms we use. Most of us have been taught that God is the head "butler." All we have to do is snap our fingers and He appears with the answer. We say, "Dear Lord, I am sick," and immediately He heals. We say, "Dear Lord, I need the rent paid," and immediately He provides the money.

True, this does work for a while. When I was first saved I would say, "Lord, here is a need," and He would immediately minister to me. I thought this was wonderful because it caused me to feel that I was becoming spiritual.

But one day it stopped, and of course I cried out, "Lord, what are you doing to me!" It was then that God began to reveal to me spiritual incompatibility.

We all know what incompatibility means to a marriage, when two are not getting along physically, emotionally or materially.

The Scripture says, "How can two walk together lest they be agreed?" Slowly I began to understand why God wants to deal with us. He wants to walk with us. In our present condition He cannot. It is as simple as that.

God met me in my sin while I was in my own Babylon of confusion. He saved me and He filled me with the Holy Spirit—but that is not the arrival point. That is the beginning.

There I was, saved in the midst of confusion, and I said, "Lord, all is wonderful," until one day the dealings of God began to manifest themselves in my life and I could not understand what was wrong. I had been taught that God was the head butler and would come when I called.

A story is told about two young boys who were getting ready to fight each other on a street corner. The father of one of the boys happened to come by. His son had his back turned, and just as the boys were getting ready to punch each other, the father gave his son a smack on the rear of his pants. The boy turned around with his fists up all ready to fight and when he saw who it was he looked very surprised and said quite timidly, "Oh, it's you, Dad!"

God does sneak up behind us sometimes when

we least expect it, and when He "smacks" us we turn around all ready to fight. I have watched many people in a real struggle with the Almighty because they could not understand that He was the one who allowed certain things to come into their lives, to break down the spiritual incompatibility.

Let's be frank. There is no time for fooling around—no time to "play church." We are kidding ourselves if we say that all good things come from God and all bad things come from the devil. That kind of theology does not go very far. We must come to an understanding of what God is trying to do in our lives.

In order to understand we must accept some changes. I was taught a great deal by my grandmother, and while I was in Bible College and seminary I also learned a great deal. But as God began to deal with me I found that much of what I had learned had to be unlearned, adjusted, or changed.

There comes a time in the life of every believer when childhood is over and the school of the Spirit begins. When this happens in your life you will find yourself asking three questions. In the first chapter of the book of Habakkuk the prophet asks, "Oh Lord, *how long* shall I cry, and thou wilt not hear!" Have you ever asked "How long, Lord?" In verse three: "*Why* dost thou show me iniquity, and cause me to behold grievance?" Have you ever asked "Why, Lord?" Why was it me who had to lose a child, a job, get my new car smashed up? And verse 13: "*Wherefore* lookest thou upon them that deal treacherously and holdeth thy tongue when the wicked devoureth the man that is more righteous than he?" Have you ever found yourself asking, "God, how can You let this condition go on? You who hate sin. How can You let those people get away with it?"

How long? Why? Wherefore? Every believer who is beginning to mature in the Spirit finds himself in circumstances in which he cries out these questions.

As we step along with the Israelites on their journey out of Babylon toward Zion, God reveals some of His answers for your life and mine.

Bob Mumford

Contents

1   *Psalm* 120   Seeing God in Things Present
2   *Psalm* 121   Learning Where to Get Your Answers
3   *Psalm* 122   Get the Proper Objectives (Recognizing God's Objectives)
4   *Psalm* 123   Learning to Wait
5   *Psalm* 124   Translating Doctrine Into Experience
6   *Psalm* 125   Becoming Established in God
7   *Psalm* 126   The Turning of the Tide
8   *Psalm* 127   Experiencing Spiritual Usefulness
9   *Psalm* 128   Experiencing Spiritual Maturity
10 *Psalm* 129   Embracing Suffering as the Balancing Factor
11 *Psalm* 130   Revealing Ourselves to Ourselves (Allowing God to reveal us to ourselves)
12 *Psalm* 131   Finding Our True Selves (and Place in the Body of Christ)
13 *Psalm* 132   Union with the Lord
14 *Psalm* 133   Union with our Brethren
15 *Psalm* 134   Bless the Lord!

15
STEPS OUT

Psalm 120

1 In my distress I cried unto the Lord and he heard me.
2 Deliver my soul, O Lord, from lying lips and from a deceitful tongue.
3 What shall be given unto thee? or what shall be done unto thee, thou false tongue?
4 Sharp arrows of the mighty, with coals of juniper!
5 Woe is me, that I sojourn in Mesech, that I dwell in the tents of Kedar!
6 My soul hath long dwelt with him that hateth peace.
7 I am for peace; but when I speak they are for war.

Seeing God in Things Present

The Psalmist begins in distress. That is where you are in Babylon, in distress. Are you saved? Have you been filled with the Holy Ghost, and yet, have you known real inner distress?

You feel it inside. I felt it, and I cried out, "God, I don't understand what is going on."

The Psalmist's eyes are being opened and he sees things that should be and are not. When you are blind; when you are not saved; not filled with the Spirit; you do not see anything; you just go along not understanding what life is all about, then one day your eyes are opened, your understanding quickened, and you see!

"In my distress I called out," said the Psalmist. Distress is something that happens. I deal with it continuously. Do you know that last year alone Americans took millions of tranquilizers? And I am sure Christians took their share also.

They are in distress because God is not doing everything that somebody told them He would do. When they snapped their fingers He did not come. When they said, "Lord, I've been on a

3

hunger strike," He did not come.

In verse two the Psalmist says, "Deliver my soul, Oh, Lord, from lying lips and from a deceitful tongue." It is not as apparent in the King James version, but the Psalmist is not referring to *his own lying* lips and deceitful tongue. He is referring to those around him.

Was there a time in your own Christian experience when you suddenly became aware of other people's sins?

You know, at first I was dealing only with my own sins, and I was getting along fairly well. Then one day God began to open my eyes and what I saw made me want to close them again. I could not stand it. I said, "Lord, did you see that Christian act like that? Did you hear that lie?"

When God wanted to get the Psalmist out of the situation he was in, God had to open his eyes to what was around him. The Psalmist was suddenly aware of other people's sins. He saw their shortcomings and their failings and he could not understand what was going on. He could not see God in things present.

What do we mean by seeing God in things present? In Romans 8:35-39 we read: "What shall separate us from the love of Christ? Shall tribulation or distress, or persecution, or famine, or nakedness, or peril, or sword?" As it is written, "For thy sake we are killed all the day long; we are accounted as sheep for the slaughter.

4

Nay, in all these things we are more than conquerors through him that loved us. For I am persuaded that neither death, nor life, nor angels, nor principalities, nor powers, *nor things present*, nor things to come, nor height, nor depth, nor any other creature shall be able to separate us from the love of God, which is in Christ Jesus, our Lord."

When I wanted to come out of confusion into God, the Lord said, "Listen, Mumford, you're going to have to learn to see God in your *present* circumstances."

I can see God in the trials I had five years ago. I remember when we didn't have any money and we were eating Cream of Wheat with canned milk. I have told about it later and said, "Hallelujah! God brought us out of that." But when I was in it I couldn't see God there. I was angry, frustrated, and distressed. I said, "God, what's the matter, why don't You put some food on the table? I'm Your servant, You've promised to take care of me!"

I could not see God in my present circumstances. I could see Him in the past, and everybody has faith for the future. Oh, one of these days it is going to be wonderful. All our troubles will be over. There is going to be a cabin in the corner of Glory Land. But now! Things are horrible! My husband is unsaved, my children are sick and the car has flat tires.

It is horrible!

Paul said, "I believe that nothing can separate me from the love of God, including the situation that I am in right now."

If I could only impart to you the ability to see that *God* has created the distress.

You say, "But you just don't understand how bad things are." I do understand. You are in distress, and I say, "Hallelujah!" How long do you want to be a baby? God creates distress to get you moving. He lets you see things around you.

I have often said, please don't let me be like those people over there! But as my eyes were opened it wasn't to condemn or confuse, only to get me moving. You can determine your own spiritual growth by your impatience with those who seem less spiritual than you.

I could see it! I dwelled with the children of Mesech in the tents of Kedar, and there was distress within me.

The Lord said, "Now do you see me in your present circumstances?" I answered, "Yes Lord, now I see it. You are doing it."

"That's right," He said. "Are you going to fight me?" "No, God."

He asked, "Why not?" I answered, "I want to come out of confusion. I'm tired of fighting."

I have fought God to a standstill because I didn't know what He was trying to do. There

6

are heelmarks every inch of the way where God has tried to get me moving.

Can you see God in your present circumstances?

One day in the midst of my distress, I closed my eyes and said, "God, I want to see You in this. Not from the past, not from the future, I want to see You right now."

When my child is sick with pneumonia I say, "God, I know You are in this thing. I know You are here and You are going to be glorified in this."

I do not want to escape. When we escape, we escape either to the past or to the future.

Remember when Jesus came to Martha and said, "If you believe, you will see the glory of God." She said, "Oh, I believe that my brother shall rise again in the day of resurrection." Jesus said, "No, Martha, I said if you believe you'll see the glory of God," and she said, "Oh, I believe if you had been there he wouldn't have died."

Jesus said, "Mary, Martha, I'm talking about *now!* Roll the stone away."

"The stone? But Lord, he stinks!"

I can't see You in this present thing Lord. In the past yes, in the future, yes, but now?

"Roll the stone away . . . Lazarus, come forth!"

Is that what You meant, Lord, when You said *if you believe* you will see the glory of God?

Psalm 121

1   *I will lift up mine eyes unto the hills. From whence does my help come?*
2   *My help cometh from the Lord, who made heaven and earth.*
3   *He will not suffer thy foot to be moved, he that keepeth thee will not slumber.*
4   *Behold, he that keepeth Israel shall neither slumber nor sleep.*
5   *The Lord is thy keeper; the Lord is thy shade upon thy right hand.*
6   *The sun shall not smite thee by day, nor the moon by night.*
7   *The Lord shall preserve thee from all evil: he shall preserve thy soul.*
8   *The Lord shall preserve thy going out and thy coming in from this time forth, and even for evermore.*

Learning Where to Get Your Answers

The Psalmist is in distress. God is trying to move him out of Babylon, and what does he do? He looks for his answers where he has always found them before.

As soon as I am in distress I know what to do. Just call a Christian friend.

"I'm in distress," I say.

"You are? I am sorry but I can't help you."

"But, you never failed me before." He says, "But I don't have anything now . . ." I try my old trusty Bible. Surely I can find my answer there. But no, nothing this time. I try the commentaries . . . nothing! I call Sister Smith. I go to a prayer meeting. Still no answer.

Once God puts you in distress you cannot get answers where you used to get them. God wants you out of confusion. He wants to teach you where to get your answers.

If you look to the hills you are going to be disappointed. I guarantee it. It does not matter where you look—to men, hills, books. You are destined for disappointment.

When God begins to mature a saint, He removes all the crutches and the props which he used for so long.

So you try your best girlfriend. She will never fail. Oh no? You call and she is suddenly cold as ice. God even deals with husbands and wives separately. Remember the time when Job needed his dear wife, what did she say? "Why don't you curse God and die!"

Have you tried going to your pastor for answers and found that he couldn't help you, either? God is trying to shut you up to Himself.

In verse two the Psalmist says, "My help cometh from the Lord."

That is not just pretty talk. My help cometh from the Lord!

Once I was moving into a parsonage. A young man who was to help me came over and said, "Pastor, I don't think I can come to paint tomorrow night." I knew he really wanted me to urge him to come, but I said, "That's all right, son. You didn't call me here, and if you don't paint it, God will send somebody else. If God doesn't send somebody else I'll do it myself." The young man looked at me, blinked a couple of times and said, "Yes, pastor, I'll be there." I did not let him think my help came from him. Because my help cometh from the Lord.

Somebody has said, "Blessed is he who expecteth nothing for he shall not be disappointed!"

If you are going to the mission field, do you

listen to those who say, "We'll be right behind you . . . we'll send you a hundred dollars every month"? The first month you get a hundred, the next month fifty, then twenty-five and so on. And you cry out to God and say, "Oh, how could those people do that to me?"

Have you wanted to get out of this religious confusion? Have you cried out and told God you are tired of looking to people, commentaries, crutches, and all kinds of systems?

Have you found that God shuts you up to Himself so that you will learn where to get your answers? So that when everything collapses around you, you can say, "Hallelujah, I learned something a while back; my answers and my help cometh from the Lord."

The word Jehovah means covenant-keeper, promise-keeper. Eight times the word is used in this Psalm. The Psalmist said his help does not come from the hills, but from the Lord, the Lord, the Lord . . . eight times. Your help comes from the promise-keeper.

He who trusts Him fully, will find Him wholly true.

Psalm 122

1   I was glad when they said unto me, Let us go into the house of the Lord.

2   Our feet shall stand within thy gates, O Jerusalem.

3   Jerusalem is builded as a city that is compact together:

4   Whither the tribes go up, the tribes of the Lord, unto the testimony of Israel, to give thanks unto the name of the Lord.

5   For there are set thrones of judgment, the thrones of the house of David.

6   Pray for the peace of Jerusalem: they shall prosper that love thee.

7   Peace be within thy walls and prosperity within thy palaces.

8   For my brethren and companions' sakes I will now say Peace be within thee.

9   Because of the house of the Lord our God, I will seek thy good.

Get the Proper Objectives
(Recognizing God's Objectives)

One of the things that has stilted and stunted and frustrated the Church has been the concept of heaven.

Yes, I believe in heaven, but heaven is not a goal, it is not an objective. Heaven is like Blue Cross and Blue Shield. If you are saved, when you die, there is no other place to go!

Some people say, "Pray for me. I only have one objective in life. I just want to make heaven my home."

What frustrating confusion! Can you imagine Paul saying; I only have one desire, to make heaven my home! There is more to this Christian life than dying!

The Psalmist says, "I was glad when they said unto me, let us go into the house of the Lord." Where is the house of the Lord?

I had been in church work for several years. I was an ordained minister, and I had prepared for the mission field. One day a young lady came to me and said, "Pastor, are you in the move of God?" I said, "Certainly, I'm in the move of God." Then I went home to my study

17

and said, "God, what is the move of God?"

I did not know whether I was in the move of God. I did not even know God was moving. All I knew was, get saved, be filled with the Holy Spirit; don't smoke, don't chew, don't run with those who do, stay holy, keep clean and wait for the Rapture.

Later I went to a camp meeting. There they asked me, "Reverend Mumford, share with us what God is saying to you."

There I was, a man 'filled with the Spirit of God,' and I got up and said, "I didn't know God was saying anything." I guess they accepted my honesty because they invited me back.

But something had gotten through to me. I turned to God and I said, "God, if You're moving, I want to know about it. I don't care what it costs. I want to know what You are doing in the earth."

This is what happened: I lost my church, my ordination, my friends. I almost lost my wife. God stripped me down to nothing, tore everything out and began to restore correct objectives in my life.

We must have definite objectives. If your objective is an eight hour day, you get tired at the seventh hour. If you know you have to work until midnight you won't get tired until 11 o'clock.

Our spiritual objectives have been confused for too long. As a child maybe you were told: "If you aren't good you won't get to heaven, if you're bad the policeman will come get you, or you will go to hell and roast forever."

I believe in heaven and in hell, but they have been terribly misused. They are *not* the objectives.

Wrong objectives continuously compound the confusion. If you don't see your goal clearly and you do not move toward it, then you will not know where you are. And you will not know how you got there because you do not know where you are going.

It is like jumping into a taxicab and saying, "Take me there!"

What is your life geared to? Do you say with the Psalmist, "I was glad when they said unto me, let us go into the house of the Lord."

Where is the house of the Lord? Hebrews 3:6 says:

"But Christ as a son over his own house, *whose house are we*, if we hold fast the confidence and the rejoicing of the hope firm unto the end."

We are Christ's house if we have the proper goal. So many people are in confusion because they do not know what God is trying to do in their lives. God is building a house and He wants to use us to make up the building.

Ephesians 2:20-22 says: "And are built upon the foundation of the apostles and prophets, Jesus Christ himself being the chief corner

19

stone; In whom all the building, *fitly framed together* groweth unto an holy temple in the Lord; In whom ye also are builded together for an habitation of God through the Spirit."

Look at Revelation, chapter 21:

"And I saw a new heaven and a new earth; for the first heaven and the first earth were passed away and there was no more sea. And I John, saw the holy city, the new Jerusalem *coming down* from God out of heaven, prepared as a bride adorned for her husband. And I heard a great voice out of heaven saying, Behold, the tabernacle of God is with men, and he will dwell with them and they shall be his people, and God himself shall be with them, and be their God. And God shall wipe away all tears from their eyes; and there shall be no more death, neither sorrow nor crying, neither shall there be any more pain; for the former things are passed away. And he that sat upon the throne said, Behold, I make all things new. [Notice He did not say that He is going to make *all new things*. He is going to make *all things new*.] And he said unto me, Write; for these words are true and faithful. And he said unto me, It is done. I am Alpha and Omega, the beginning and the end. I will give unto him that is athirst of the fountain of the water of life freely. He that overcometh shall inherit all things, and I will be his God and he shall be my son . . . And there came unto me one of the seven angels which had the seven vials full of the seven last plagues, and talked with me, saying: Come hither, I will show thee the bride, the Lamb's wife. And he carried me away in the spirit to a great and high mountain, and showed me that great city, the holy Jerusalem descending out of heaven from God. Having the glory of God . . ."

I was glad when finally one day I began to understand what the move of God in the earth and in my life was all about. I wish I had deeper understanding of His plan and purposes. But I do understand this: The House of the Lord (Ephesians 2 and Hebrews 3:6) is that Jerusalem, the bride, the city of our God. And He is building that house NOW!

The new Jerusalem is being built now. And of what is it being built? Living stones. You and me.

A pile of stones does not make a building. A minister asked me to come and see his church. He had 1200 members, he said. So I went. But I didn't see a church. I saw 1200 stones. I said, "Beautiful stones, when are you going to start building?"

He said, "What do you mean?" I said, "The stones have to be chipped, fitted and builded." He said, "You should meet Sister Smith, she is very spiritual." I said, "She is? Who is she spiritual with?"

It is easy to be spiritual all by yourself. When I am in the shower I am the best singer. But when I hear a great voice, I say, "Well, perhaps singing is not my calling." We have to be properly fitted together to make a building. Each in our own place.

What are some proper objectives in our lives?
1. To know that there is a moving in the earth
2. To know that God is building a house
3. To be a living stone
4. To be builded on top, between and beneath other stones

Do not try to be spiritual all by yourself. The only way you can truly grow and develop in God and come out of spiritual confusion is to be builded together under God.

My heart aches to be builded with other brethren. I am not a lone ranger. I am only one stone who seeks to find its place in the building of God.

I have found my goal. I have not reached it, but I have found it. I want to be what God called me to be before the foundation of the world.

First there was the Tabernacle and then there was the Temple. Now God is building a New Temple. A living Temple for His own habitation, built of living stones, that He might dwell in it through the Holy Spirit.

"Our feet shall stand within thy gates, Oh Jerusalem." That is a true goal. It is something that God is doing *now* in the lives of many men and women.

When we cease trying to build our own little Kingdom, God begins to build His in us.

Psalm 123

1 Unto thee lift I up mine eyes, O thou that dwellest in the heavens.
2 Behold as the eyes of servants look unto the hand of their masters, and as the eyes of a maiden unto the hand of her mistress; so our eyes wait upon the Lord our God until he have mercy upon us.
3 Have mercy upon us, O Lord, have mercy upon us; for we are exceedingly filled with contempt.
4 Our soul is exceedingly filled with the scorning of those that are at ease and with the contempt of the proud.

Learning to Wait

Most people cannot stand waiting. Your husband drops you off at the shopping center and says he will be back for you in an hour and then comes back in two hours. You probably would wait and stew and fuss the whole extra hour.

If you are ever going to come out of confusion into God, you are going to have to learn the secret of waiting on God for His timing. To hurry God is to find fault with Him. For God is never late, but He does not always come when you want Him to.

Have you ever found yourself angry with God, provoked or frustrated because He did not do what you thought He ought to do when you thought He ought to do it? You say, "God, what is the matter with You, why don't You heal her now?"

The Psalmist has now learned where to find his answers. "Unto thee do I lift up mine eyes." He is not looking to the hills any more. God is telling him something important. Let me give you an illustration.

Picture a great monarch sitting on his throne

surrounded by much splendor. He has many men around him, and one of them is named Bob Mumford, and he says: "King, oh King, is there anything you want me to do for you? I am ready to do anything for you. Do you need preaching done? I will do it, anything King, I am ready to go . . ." The king looks at me patiently and after a while he turns to one of the others and says:

"Please quiet that man—I will call him when I need him."

For years I was just like that. I persisted in my requests of God. I had the preacher's itch. I wanted to be used, and when I came home they gave me an usher's band. I thought, "What is the matter with these people? Don't they recognize a good preacher when they see one?"

Then one day God showed me that I was like a Western Union boy. Can you see me sitting in the outer office? Every so often I jump up out of my chair.

"Boss, are there any messages? Did anything come over the wires? Boss, I'll go, I'll go, I'll get on my bicycle Boss, if you need any messages taken, I'll deliver."

With amazing patience the Boss says: "Will you be still. When a message comes I will give it to you and you can deliver it."

Look at the Psalm again, verse 2: "Behold, as the eyes of the servants look unto the hand of

28

their master." Can you imagine the servant sitting or kneeling before his master's throne . . . waiting! Isn't that horrible. I would rather do anything than wait.

Have you ever heard somebody in the church say, "Let's do something, even if it is wrong!" If you want to know compounded confusion, just get up and run when the Master has not given the word.

One of the most necessary lessons we have to learn if we are to come out of confusion is how to wait on the beck and call of the Master.

You have seen two extreme degrees of failure in this realm. Some people sit down and say, "Well, if God wants to use me He knows where I am." That is not waiting. The other one tears the door right off the hinges. They do not knock, they rush in and mess up everything.

Somebody has said, "Patience is a virtue, possess it if you can; seldom found in women, never found in men." As an Englishman, I have no patience at all. Put me in a supermarket on a Saturday afternoon with all those people pushing and shoving grocery carts and I will soon be like a volcano ready to erupt. But I am learning. Learning what it means to wait on God's timing.

If I take you fifty miles out to sea and put you on a buoy and say, "Wait for me, I'll be back soon," . . . when I come back three days later you will still be there because you could not go anywhere. If I let you off in downtown Los Angeles and said, "Wait for me," you would wait for a few minutes, maybe an hour, then hop in a taxicab.

One of the greatest traps Christians fall into is this: if God does not come when they think He should, they do it themselves.

Have you ever planned a city-wide campaign? Maybe somebody says, "I don't think God is in this," and you say, "Well, if He isn't, we'll do it ourselves."

Sure you can have a city-wide campaign without God. You can build a church without God. Many people do it. Get some planners, some door-bell ringers, a contractor.

If your child is sick, do you say, "Lord, I am going to pray for him, and if You do not heal him I will take him to the hospital." Now if you were out on that buoy with a sick child . . . with no one around . . . you would have to trust God.

If you can do it yourself, who needs God? If you have Blue Cross-Blue Shield, 100,000 dollars, a split-level house and two cars in the garage, who needs God? I'll do it myself!

One of the surest ways to spare yourself much of the painful dealings of God is to learn that little word *dependence*.

Do you know why I do not do it myself? I need Jesus. I am not playing games when I say that. I *need* Him.

When God stops, I stop. If He does not have anything to say, that makes two of us. I will tell you where God tested me on this. I was in a meeting in New England. I taught for a week and it was glorious. God used me, people were getting blessed and healed and the place was packed to the door every night. The final day came. I sought the Lord all afternoon; prayed, fasted, but nothing came. I said to myself, the Lord has done this before, he will give me some Scripture and a message during the song service preceding my teaching. I came to the song service, nothing happened. During the offering I started to go through my Bible to warm something up. I thought: we'll have left-overs. But I couldn't find anything. That whole Bible was dry, the pages just stared back at me.

Finally they introduced me and I thought, the Lord will give me a word as I walk up to the pulpit, He's waited this long before. I got up to the pulpit and just stood there, a complete blank. Here it was, the final night of a big week and the teacher comes into the pulpit with absolutely nothing to say! So I just stood there, and finally I said, "I don't know what to say!"

The pastor was sitting down in a pew and I said to him, "Pastor, what shall I do?" He said, "I don't know." So I turned my eyes from him and looked over the congregation, and as I did he jumped up from his seat and began to prophesy, "Thou hast seen an object lesson this night," he said. "It is not of man that runneth or man that willeth, but God that showeth mercy."

I had been the object lesson.

After the prophesy I waited. Still nothing came to my mind. There was a lady sitting in the back with a big black hat on. She looked very chic. I looked at her and the Lord said, "Ask that lady to play the piano." I did not even know if she could play. I looked at her and said, "Lady, back there with the black hat, would you play something for us, please?" She looked at me, took off that big hat and came walking up the aisle. It was so quiet in there that you could hear the people breathing.

She sat down at the piano, and as she touched the keys, the glory of God filled the church. It was beautiful. It turned out that she was a Christian who had fallen away and God reclaimed her that night as she sat at the piano playing to His glory.

I was still standing in the pulpit. Everybody was crying and I had not said a word yet! When the meeting was over I said "Amen!" and that was all the part I had that night.

A few years ago, if God had not come, I would have said, "God, if You don't have anything to do or say, I'll just take care of the sermon myself."

Most of the dealings of God are designed to bring about a dependence on Him. Do you know why God asks for the tithe? If you make a hundred dollars a week and your bills are a hundred and five, what do you do? Do you say, "God, You want me to pay my bills, don't You?" But when you take that ten out and drop it in the plate in church you are really saying to God: "This ten-dollar bill is my evidence to You that I really need You."

We must wait on God's timing. Samuel said to Saul: "Wait here until I get back in seven days." Saul said, "Yes, sir, I'll do it." Samuel went away and Saul waited. One, two, three . . . seven days. The people were impatient. "Look," they said, "the Philistines are all out here . . . let's sacrifice to God." And so Saul finally ordered the sacrifice brought in; they sacrificed, and there was Samuel.

"Saul, what have you done!" He took off his mantle, ripped it down the middle, and said, "Thus shalt Jehovah do for the Kingdom is rent from thee this day."

Because he did not wait, Saul missed the purposes of God.

God is never late . . . but He never comes on your time.

He has His reasons. He is doing something in us while we wait.

Read Exodus 24:12: "And the Lord said unto Moses, 'Come up to me into the mount and *be there.*'" What does He want Moses to do? Just be

33

there. Can you hear Moses fretting? "Lord, I don't mind coming up; what do you want me to do? Here I am Lord, ready to go, send me Lord." And God says: "Moses, Moses, just come up and *be* there. Don't do anything, don't say anything, don't pray for grandmother, don't worry about the rent, don't worry about anti-Christ, just come up and wait."

That is the hardest assignment you will ever have.

. . . "Come up and be there and I will give thee tables of stone . . . And Moses went up into the mount and a cloud covered the mount. And the glory of the Lord abode upon Mount Sinai, and the cloud covered it six days; and the seventh day he called unto Moses out of the midst of the cloud . . ." It took seven days before God spoke a word. And what did Moses do all this time? He just waited. And I think that by now he had learned something about waiting. What was God doing those six days?

He was conditioning the human faculty to receive from God. The waiting time is a conditioning that prepares the human spirit to receive what God wants to give you.

Most of us could never receive what God wants to give us until He has put us through a time of waiting.

While Moses was up on the mountain his people were waiting below. What were they doing?

This is the difference between spirituality and mere religious activity. When the people had waited for a while they grew impatient. They gathered around Aaron and said: "We don't have a God; let's make one. Let's do something, even if it is wrong." And Aaron went along with them.

That is religious confusion.

While we are waiting, God allows time for the restless agitation of our spirit to settle down.

Psalm 37:7 says: "Rest in the Lord and wait patiently for him; fret not thyself because of him who prospereth in his way, because of the man who bringeth wicked devices to pass . . ."

A lady came one day, all upset. "Reverend Mumford," she said, "I can't find God anymore. I am confused. I used to walk with Him but now I don't know where He is." She was quite agitated and I told her: "Lady, sit down, and be quiet. Let us just sit here in the study for a few moments. You remind me of a fishbowl in which there is a lot of sand. You are all stirred up, and the sand and the fish are all mixed together and you say, 'I don't know where the fish are.' When you set the bowl down the sand will settle and there are all the fish."

Most people could find God and hear His voice if they would just sit down, be quiet, and let their human spirit settle. As long as you are running in circles God could not speak to you if

He wanted to, because you would not know His voice.

God often speaks to me just as I am coming out of sleep in the morning. That is when my human spirit is most quiet.

While I was preparing for the mission field I worked in a hospital. One night a young man pulled into the emergency-ward parking area with tires screeching. His dad just had a heart attack in the car and was dying. The nurse and I ran to the car and the boy was in hysterics. He screamed, "Do something, do something!" Finally I said:

"Be quiet, do you want me to get as excited as you are, then neither of us can do anything?"

This is how some people behave with God. They say, "Do something, do something." Do you know that the heated human spirit can cause more confusion than any demon?

There is another reason for keeping us waiting.

Habakkuk 2:20 says: "But the Lord is in his holy temple, let all the earth keep silence before him."

We Christians have lost our sense of reverence. We need to discover God's presence and majesty. We need to wait before Him.

Psalm 124

1 If it had not been the Lord who was on our side, now may Israel say;
2 If it had not been the Lord who was on our side, when men rose up against us:
3 Then they had swallowed us up quick, when their wrath was kindled against us:
4 Then the waters had overwhelmed us, the stream had gone over our soul:
5 Then the proud waters had gone over our soul.
6 Blessed be the Lord, who hath not given us as a prey to their teeth.
7 Our soul is escaped as a bird out of the snare of the fowlers: the snare is broken, and we are escaped.
8 Our help is in the name of the Lord, who made heaven and earth.

Translating Doctrine Into Experience

Many people have a lot of doctrine in their heads. They know all about it; they can quote it. But getting the doctrine from the head into the heart is a frightening experience.

You cannot really know anything until you have proved it to yourself.

Remember the man who who tried to cast out demons in "the name of Jesus whom Paul preaches." It did not work.

What you say has no power until *you* know it is true.

There is a story about a man who was about to cross over the Niagara Falls on a bicycle. There was a wire stretched out across the gully and the man turned to an on-looker and said: "Do you believe I can ride this bicycle across the wire to the other side?" "I believe you can," said the other fellow. "Then get on!" said the man.

We say, "Yes, Lord I believe—from my head up." And God says: "If you believe, then get on the bike!" "But I'm scared, God." He says, "That's right, but it is only as you translate what you know into experience that it does any good."

Surely, you have heard preaching that was dead and on another occasion preaching that brought forth life. What makes the difference? The first fellow did not know what he was talking about; the second had really experienced it.

This is often hard to understand. First God brings you to a commitment. You say, "Yes, God, I will trust You with my health, my finances, my family, my job." Then God works that commitment out in your life. Someone said: "God extracts from us in a time of war what we promised Him in the time of peace."

When everything is rosy it is easy to say, "Lord, I trust You for my material needs." God says, "Wonderful, I heard that." After a while there is going to be an experience where you can translate what you have said down into your heart.

And so you lose your job, the bank account you kept just in case the Lord would not come through on His promises dwindles down to nothing, and God says, "Now do you trust Me?"

I have trusted the Lord for my body for thirteen years. I very seldom go to a doctor. But there have been times when God has tested me.

Today I say Jesus Christ is the Healer. I do not say that because I read a book about healing; I *know* Jesus Christ is the Healer, that He provides for all my needs. I have had opportunities to translate my doctrine into experience.

What I know has become my very own.

Let us not labor under any false delusions. We are in a real battle. The devil and demons are real. The trials and the wilderness we go through are real. This is not what we call in the Navy a "dry run," a practice run. God is not practicing on you. This is the real thing.

The Psalmist says: "If the Lord had not been on our side I would have gone under."

If the Lord had not helped me I would have gone under. Because every time I went through a trial I failed. I said, "God, I don't understand. How many times can a man fail and You still love him?"

In the early years of ministry all I knew was weakness, failure, and defeat. I was so impatient with my own spirit. Finally God spoke one day; "I am seeking to translate the doctrines you know into a reality in your own spirit. The Word must become flesh and dwell in you."

This is no dry run. If you miss it, your bones are liable to bleach in the wilderness.

I have seen good men and women go down because they did not understand that God was trying to get the doctrine from their heads into their hearts.

In verse seven the Psalmist says: "Our soul is escaped, like a bird out of the snare of the fowler."

41

It is one thing for you to be escaped; it is another thing to know that the snare has been broken. What is the snare?

In Colossians 2:15 Paul says: "And, having spoiled principalities and powers, He [Jesus Christ] made a show of them openly, triumphing over them in it."

I believe with all my heart that the devil is defeated. Jesus is the king of the earth!

Satan has no power except the power of deception. Do you know why I can preach that way? Why I can stand and declare to you that the snare is broken? Because he has tried to trap me again many times, and I remind him: "You cannot put that snare back on me, it is broken."

I stood on a street corner waiting for a bus one day. I had been a Christian for five years and was in the ministry. Next to me stood a man smoking. The smoke went under my nose and I was suddenly filled with a desire for a cigarette. My mouth began to water . . . then I remembered, and said: "Devil, you cannot trap me again, because the snare has been broken."

One evangelist told it this way. When he was a boy his parents owned a grocery store in a small town. Farmers used to bring in chickens to trade for salt and flour. The farmer would get up early in the morning, catch four or five chickens, bind their legs together and carry them to town that way. After they were weighed, he would get his pen-knife and cut the strings that bound the chickens together. He said: "I would lay the chickens on the ground and after I had cut the string they just stayed, in the same position. 'Shoo, chickens, you are free,' but they would just lie there. They had been bound so long they did not know they were free. Then I would do what any red-blooded boy would do, I would kick those chickens and they would fly screaming."

I am convinced that God permits the devil to give you a "good swift kick" just so you will know those strings are broken.

When were our strings cut? When were we healed, when were we delivered, when were we saved? On Calvary. Jesus did it for us.

Jesus said: "The Spirit of the Lord is upon me, I came to proclaim deliverance and the loosing of the bonds to the captives . . . I came to tell people they have been freed."

I watch people who have been cut loose just lie there and say, "I'm bound, please pray for me." My response is: "You are not bound, the only thing that keeps you is the habit. You have been bound for so long you don't know what freedom is." Sometimes when people are healed or saved it doesn't make sense to them for a while. They cannot really believe they

43

are free.

It is important for you to know that the snare is broken. You need to experience it for yourself; you need to know it for others so that you can help them see.

The Psalmist says, "Our help is in the name of the Lord." We say, "In the name of Jesus," and sometimes nothing happens. Why? Isn't there power in the name?

The name is not a magic want. If it does not really mean anything to you, it will not mean anything to the demons to whom you are talking.

I learned a lesson some time ago. The Psalmist says: "Yea, though I walk through the valley of the shadow of death I will fear no evil, for thou art with me. Thy rod [which is authority] and thy staff [which is guidance] they comfort me" . . . and suddenly I realized that we do not learn to use the name of Jesus until we really have to. Not until we walk through the valley. We do not learn until we get into a situation in which we are forced to use it.

The only way you are ever going to appropriate the name of Jesus for your own is when you stop trying to escape a difficult situation by running some place else for help.

Somebody has said that the devil is like a little puppy dog. You say, "Puppy, go home," and he keeps on following you. Then one day you say, with authority, "Puppy go home or else!" and he runs because he knows you mean it.

Once while working in a candy factory between college semesters, I was cleaning out sticky candy from a big tank, and the temperature in there must have been 240 degrees. I was sweating and miserable and mean, and the Accuser had been on my back all day long. He said, "You failed God, that's why you are in here. You will sweat and you will die, and you will never be in the ministry because you are a misfit and you never have been any good." Finally I came out of that candy tank, and in desperation I said: "IN THE NAME OF JESUS, LEAVE ME ALONE!" And to my surprise, he left!

I believe that God puts you in more than one situation trying to teach you how to use that *name*. But as long as you run to somebody else you will never learn. It must become your own.

Our help is in the name of the Lord. I believe it is one of the greatest heritages Christ has given to His Church. I love the name of Jesus. I live it, I breathe it. I have learned to use it when Satan tries to throw that broken snare back over me.

The enemy says, "You're caught!" and I say, "You're a liar! In the name of Jesus, get that snare off my back."

The snare has been broken, not only for you,

but for husbands, for wives, for those to whom you minister. When we stand in the name of Jesus . . . who can stand before us?

Psalm 125

1 They that trust in the Lord shall be as mount
   Zion, which cannot be removed, but abid-
   eth forever.
2 As the mountains are round about Jerusalem,
   so the Lord is round about his people from
   henceforth and even forever.
3 For the rod of the wicked shall not rest upon
   the lot of the righteous; lest the righteous
   put forth their hands unto iniquity.
4 Do good, O Lord, unto those that be good,
   and to them that are upright in their hearts.
5 As for such as turn aside unto their crooked
   ways, the Lord shall lead them forth with
   the workers of iniquity, but peace shall be
   upon Israel.

Becoming Established in God

I have served on various mission boards examining missionary candidates who wanted to be ordained or licensed to preach the Gospel. It is important to find out if the man or woman is established in God. "Established" means to be settled, strengthened. Such candidates have moved into God and you know they are not flighty. They are not blown by every wind of doctrine.

This chapter's psalm opens with an interesting verse: "They that *trust* in the Lord shall be as mount Zion, which cannot be removed." They will be solid, established. This is something God wants to do with every believer. Consider the word *trust*. I had been in the ministry for a long time before I began to understand that there is a difference between trusting and believing. I always used to say when things got a little rough, "I believe, I believe," and I really did not believe.

This is mental gymnastics. When you say "I believe, I believe," with your mind, your heart replies, "You're a liar." You try to do something with your mind and your heart will not agree. In studying both the Hebrew and Greek grammars, I found that when God uses the word *trust*, that is exactly what He means. When He means *believe*, He uses the word believe.

Believe is a verb and it is active. When God says He wants you to believe, He requires that you do something.

But there are times when we simply cannot believe. God knows this. That is why He sometimes says very plainly that He wants us to trust.

God knows how we really feel, and the sooner we can be honest about it, the better. You say, "I believe, I believe," and God replies, "Do you?"

When you cannot believe, you still can trust.

"Trust in the Lord and lean not to thine own understanding."

Trusting means, "I do not understand what God is doing; I cannot figure it out. I do not know what He is doing in this circumstance, but I can say: God, I know one thing. I know who You are. I know Your character. You are not going to hurt me and You will never do me wrong; so even if I do not understand, I will trust You!"

Trust is passive, rooted in the integrity of God.

When you see a man planting his feet solidly on the rock, getting ready to do some trusting, you see someone who is becoming established

50

and settled in God.

When I was in Bogota, Colombia, teaching a training course, God began to work on me, causing terrible pressure. Finally I said, "God, what do You want, what are You trying to tell me?" And God impressed on me that He wanted me to go to school. If He had said Iceland or Mongolia I would have been ready to go. But school!

I couldn't believe it, but the feeling persisted, and finally God gave me the name of the school—an Episcopal seminary. And me a Pentecostal! I can tell you I went through some mental gymnastics until God had truly convinced me.

At last I said: "I do not understand, God, and I cannot imagine how You are going to work out the practical details. I do not even have faith to believe it can be done. But from this day on, God, I am going to trust You to work it out, to reveal Your purpose and plan for my life."

There is a story about a merchant who told his little son to climb up on an eight-foot ladder. Then he told his son to jump. "Daddy, will you catch me?" he asked. The boy jumped, the father stepped back and the boy hit the concrete. The father said: "Son, that'll teach you never to trust anybody."

Now, we are not recommending this man nor his method, but the story makes a point. The boy jumped because he trusted his father. If you want to come out of confusion, you must learn to take a jump in the dark on pure trust.

You will have to say: "God, I do not understand, but if You want me to jump off this eight-foot ladder, here I come."

Three inches from the floor is where He usually catches you!

It is rare to find someone who is established in God. Because people do not learn how to trust. They are always trying to believe, trying to produce.

Faith is a gift of God, it is born of God, but there are times when God requires that you trust Him. Trust His character, His nature; without seeing, without believing, without understanding. He just says, "Trust Me."

When you learn to trust there is a settling factor in your life, and you suddenly find yourself becoming established.

"They that trust in the Lord shall be as mount Zion, which cannot be removed . . ." The man who trusts in God will find God faithful.

In verse four the Psalmist in this chapter continues, "Do good, O Lord, unto those who are good, and to those that be good and . . . upright in their hearts. As for such as turn aside unto their crooked ways. *The Lord* shall lead them forth [you should not think that the devil is doing it!] with the workers of iniquity . . ."

Over the years I have watched good Christian workers, people who love the Lord and whom

God has used, get caught up in some deception. When we talk about deception we mean believing a lie.

There comes a time when God wants you to take on added responsibility. I used to try to make people feel good even when they were not good. God said, "Preach, telling them to *be* good, then they will *feel* good." Some people try to get the feeling without being.

God, however, expects you to take on added responsibility. He will not expect anything from you that you cannot do. But He does expect some things.

"Do good, O Lord, unto them that are upright in their hearts," says the Psalmist. Whether you are upright in your heart is something only God can know about you. You can deceive your wife, you can deceive the world, you can even deceive yourself. But you cannot deceive God.

We are discussing an increase in responsibility. You cannot cheat, lie or deceive; you cannot put on a false front before God.

"Whatsoever a man sows . . ." I have seen how it works. There are those who are paralyzed by fear at the thought of standing up in a meeting to testify. I thought, "Lord, why?" And He replied, "Observe." So I began to observe. When some person got up to testify, one could overhear such remarks as, "Look at that hairdo," "Look at that dress." I realized why they were afraid to testify: their own weakness was at the root of their accusation. What you sow you reap.

I give the enemy less and less credit in my theology. What I see is Jesus giving men their just reward according to the law of sowing and reaping.

Some people go on detours of many-years' duration, into false and difficult dealings due to self-deception.

Do you know that it is possible to walk from Egypt to Canaan in a matter of eight days? It took the Israelites 40 years to pass through the wilderness. You can move quickly from confusion into God if you know and understand what is going on.

Will you join with David in Psalm 18:19-26 where he says,

"He brought me forth also into a large place, he delivered me, because he delighted in me. The Lord rewarded me according to my righteousness; according to the cleanness of my hands hath he recompensed me. For I have kept the ways of the Lord, and I have not wickedly departed from my God. For all his ordinances were before me, and I did not put away his statutes from me. I was also upright before him, and I kept myself from mine iniquity. Therefore hath the

Lord recompensed me according to my righteousness, according to the cleanness of mine hands in his eyesight. With the merciful thou wilt show thyself merciful, with an upright man thou will show thyself upright; with the pure thou wilt show thyself pure; froward thou wilt show thyself froward."

A froward man is one who takes the truth and twists it to his own advantage. Have you ever heard a man and a wife each tell their version of a family quarrel? He tells his side and she tells hers, and it sounds like two different marriages.

The theme of deception goes through the whole Bible. Look at 1 Cor. 3:16, 17. "Know ye not [ye is plural, not singular here] that ye are the temple and that the Spirit of God dwelleth in you? If any man defile [mar, corrupt or deceive] the temple, him shall God destroy [the same Greek word that was translated defile earlier in the verse]."

When you double-deal with God's finances, when you pretend to prophesy, when you put on a hypocritical front, when you try to look like something you are not, then you are sowing deception. And he who sows deception will reap the same and suddenly find himself deceived.

Some people think they are getting away with it when they toy with another's wife or husband, deal dishonestly with money, hurt others' reputations, and so on.

The issue is not salvation. Salvation is by grace. We are talking about coming out of confusion. We are talking about a maturing believer. Can you say to God, "Deal with me according to the cleanness of my hands—in Your eyes."

I have tried under God to keep my hands, my life, my mind, my mouth, my ministry clean. Not because of people—I could deceive you. Not because of my wife, I could deceive her. But because there is One who knows all things.

Hebrews 4:13 says, ". . . but all things are naked and open unto the eyes of him with whom we have to do." The word naked comes from a word that means to stretch forth the neck. In other words, God has you stretched out and wide open.

I have watched people deceive. A missionary friend of mine traveled miles on the turnpike to speak in a large church. They announced that the offering would be for the missionary, and about 200 dollars came in. After the meeting my friend went by the pastor's house. The pastor stuck an envelope in his hand and shoved him out the door. In the envelope my friend found $15.00. He was crushed.

But I know Who keeps the books.

He who seeks to deceive the temple of God, him shall God deceive, destroy, corrupt.

If you are going to grow in God you must learn

to play the game very carefully. When somebody short-changes you at the supermarket you say, "You didn't give me enough change." But what do you say if they give you an extra dollar?

Once while helping a friend in a gas station a man pulled up in a truck. "Give me two dollars' worth of gas and a slip for four dollars." Looking him straight in the eye, I said, "I wouldn't sell myself for two dollars." He was so angry I thought he was going to punch me. He had always done it that way . . . many people do. Padded expense accounts. Trying to deceive others, financially, materially, spiritually.

Do not try to impress people. Be yourself under God for there is One who knows what you really are.

This may not be popular teaching. But why are our mental institutions packed full of people? Why do people consume tons of tranquilizers? Yet the minute the drug wears off the hand of God is still upon them.

I do not expect to have a nervous breakdown. I plan to be full of joy, peace, and righteousness that God offers through the Holy Spirit. Because when the checker at the grocery store gives me an extra dollar I cannot take it home. It does not belong to me.

The other day someone introduced me as "Doctor" Mumford. I said, "Me, a doctor?" I could not let that go. I am not a doctor and cannot put on a show.

It is worth considering, who does the reaping, and who does the deceiving?

Psalm 126

1 When the Lord turned again the captivity of
   Zion, we were like them that dream.
2 Then was our mouth filled with laughter, and
   our tongue with singing: then said they
   among the heathen, The Lord hath done
   great things for them.
3 The Lord hath done great things for us;
   whereof we are glad.
4 Turn again our captivity, O Lord, as the
   streams in the south.
5 They that sow in tears shall reap in joy.
6 He that goeth forth and weepeth, bearing
   precious seed, shall doubtless come again
   with rejoicing, bringing his sheaves with
   him.

The Turning of the Tide

Have you ever gone through an experience so glorious that you had to pinch yourself to see if it was really true?

This last year I have often said to my wife, "I'm so happy it is almost illegal."

There has been such joy in the Lord, in ministry and in the love of Jesus that it has seemed like a dream at times. This is the normal Christian life as God would have us live it.

Of course I have troubles surrounding me.

But the Lord has turned my captivity and I am like them that dream.

The turning of the captivity does something inside a man. The Psalmist says, "Our mouth was filled with laughter and our tongue with singing," but notice where the Psalmist and his people were: still in captivity among the heathen.

How does God turn our captivity? Look at John 7:37, 38. "In the last day, that great day of the feast, Jesus stood and cried out, "If any man thirst, let him come unto me and drink . . . Out of his heart shall flow rivers of living water."

First we drink and drink and drink . . . then one day, out of our hearts shall flow rivers. That is the turning of our captivity, the turning of the tide.

God has provided drink for everyone, He pours of Himself to us. But if there does not come a time in your life when the tide turns within you and begins to flow out to others, you will remain in confusion.

I stood on the seashore and watched the tide go out. At one particular moment the tide turned and began to flow back in. Scientists can pinpoint the exact moment when the tide will turn each day.

God knows each of us, and He knows we each have different needs. Some of us need to drink more of the things of God. But there comes a time when we have drunk enough. Now it is time to let some of those blessings flow through us to others. It is time to start helping others, to minister to them.

Spiritual maturity is when you begin to produce more than you consume. Most Christians are consumers. Few ever experience the joy of being producers.

If the tide doesn't turn in your life, you will remain in confusion. Everything God pours into you just stays there and eventually grows stagnant. I once heard someone point out the difference between the Sea of Galilee and the

Dead Sea. Both are fed by the river Jordan, but the Sea of Galilee is filled with fish, while nothing can live in the Dead Sea. The difference is that the Sea of Galilee has both an inflow and an outflow, whereas nothing flows out of the Dead Sea. It is a dead end.

Just as there must be a turning of the tide in your own life, an inflow and an outflow, so must there be a turning of the tide in your church.

There are Christian churches who drink and drink, and when there is no turning of the tide, no outlet, they begin to fight with each other.

If God can turn the tide in my life and in my church, then I know He can turn it in my nation also. I believe there is going to be a revival in this nation and I do not think we will have to wait very long to see it.

Someone said to me, "Would you like to be in heaven?" I said, "No thanks! I'd rather be here." I have heard people say they were homesick for heaven, but every time they were sick and it looked as if they might go there, they wanted prayer for healing. To say you are homesick for heaven is just religious talk. God wants to change you inside so that you don't want to leave here until it is His time.

Numbers 14:21 is God's promise to us; in fact, it is His oath: "But as truly as I live [and that is surely truly!] all the earth shall be filled with the Glory of God."

I don't want to go to heaven (yet). I want to see God's glory fill the earth, cities and nations brought to God. I want to see God's visitation upon the earth.

The visitation upon the earth only comes as the tide is turned in *you* as an individual, in your church and in the nation, so that the earth may be filled with His glory.

This is God's promise, and I believe it whether my generation will see it or not.

Psalm 127

1 Except the Lord build the house, they labor in vain that build it; except the Lord keep the city, the watchman waketh but in vain.
2 It is vain for you to rise up early, to sit up late, to eat the bread of sorrows; for so he giveth his beloved sleep.
3 Lo, children are an heritage from the Lord; and the fruit of the womb is his reward.
4 As arrows are in the hand of a mighty man; so are children of the youth.
5 Happy is the man that hath his quiver full of them; they shall not be ashamed, but they shall speak with the enemies in the gate.

Experiencing Spiritual Usefulness

Do you know the difference between religion and spirituality? Religion comes from a Latin word which means to "tie back " It is man's effort to tie himself back to God

What God does is spiritual.

Religious activity is often fruitless, it can be damaging, it may be worse than nothing.

Jesus couldn't deal with the religious people in His day. They could not see their need for Him. Christians today can become very religious too, inwardly and outwardly.

"Except the Lord build the house [That is spiritual], they labor in vain that build it [That's religious]."

You can build a three-million-dollar church building without God. Many people do it, and God is nowhere around. It happens all over America and it is frightening.

Once I built a church. I dug a hole fifty feet wide, and 75 feet long I had $300, and God told me to dig that hole. After paying the man with the bulldozer $150, I had $150 left.

The next morning I went down into that hole

and said, "God, if You don't put a church in this hole, You had better bury me in it."

Don't ever dig a hole unless God tells you to.

So there I was in the hole, and a contractor came up and said "I understand you are building a church?" "Yes," I replied, and he said, "How much do you think it is going to cost you?"

In my mind I was considering $10,000, and the contractor said, "I'd say $150,000 at least!" I leaned up against a tree and almost fainted.

Later, I went to the bank to borrow three thousand dollars to lay the foundation. I had all the papers signed, and as I walked into the bank God said: "Don't borrow any money." I had to tell the banker I didn't want his money. I told him that God had impressed us to build the church on a pay-as-you-go basis.

On the way home, I bought $100 worth of concrete and spent the other fifty on odds and ends. There I was, flat broke and all we had was a big hole and a little bit of concrete.

I stood by that hole and wondered how God was going to erect a building there. A man drove up and got out of his car. I'd never seen him before. He walked over to me and said, "What are you doing, preacher?" I answered, "I'm building a church."

He looked at the hole for a little while and I could see tears come into his eyes. Then he took something out of his pocket and handed it to me. Off he drove and when I looked in my hand, there was a $100 bill!

I could feel my own eyes fill with tears. "Thank you, Lord, for the confirmation."

Christianity is based on supernaturalism. God works in ways that are mysterious and supernatural to man.

When our church was half-way up I said: "Lord, we need 130 twenty-two-foot timbers." Soon after I went to preach in a nearby town, and the pastor there told me that they were tearing down a high school. I went over to see, and there were my timbers. Of course I had expected them clean and delivered on a truck to our church, but instead there they were, rafters in an attic.

All the men in the church got together, brought the timbers down, took out all the nails and built us a church!

Day by day God provided the things we needed. When we were laying blocks we needed a carpenter to build a door frame. A man came walking up to me and said "I don't like it, but God sent me!" He was a carpenter, and he helped us through the rest of the building program."

One day while standing inside the half-finished building (the floor, sides, and the roof were completed), I said, "God, truly You are building this house." The presence of God came into that place so strongly that I could feel His manifest presence, and tears filled my eyes.

God made me to know, "If I do not build the house, I am not obligated to fill it." I said, "Lord, I've felt You here from the beginning." He said, "I'll build it, and I'll fill it."

There have been churches filled with the presence of God. I have seen them grow and have seen the members decide to build a larger building. But when they moved into the new building, God stayed behind.

Please do not get involved in anything in which you do not have evidence that God is in. If you feel God wants you to do something, say, "Lord, how do I know that You are present?" And when He opens up the way or closes the door, say, "Thank you, Lord, for the evidence."

If you do not have evidence that God is present in a project, for His sake, stay out of it. Get away from it, because it is only religious. That which is merely religious will run you in circles. And when you are through running you will be nowhere.

That which is born of God is *spiritual*, and God will take care of it.

The Psalmist says, "It is vain for you to rise up early, to sit up late and eat the bread of sorrow." That motivation is religious.

A friend of mine in seminary used to set his

alarm clock for 4 A.M. Thus he could get up and be the first light on, so that others when they would look out their windows would see that he was up first and would think he was very spiritual. That smacks of religion.

I have been through this, too. I have fasted long, and all I got was skinny! Like Martin Luther, trying to beat myself with chains so that I could become spiritual.

It is vain for you to try to make yourself look holy. Holiness is not looking; holiness is being. A friend of mine was graduated from Bible school, and when I saw him he didn't have a tie on. I looked at him and said, "What happened?" "Brother," he replied, "we can't have those vain things!"

If you are in bondage to a necktie you need deliverance! If you think that your dress, or your hair-do, or your fasting, or your prayers add anything to your salvation, then you do not understand anything of the grace of Jesus Christ.

As long as you stay in religious confusion, you are not going to become spiritual by staying up all hours. Look at Moffatt's translation of the last part of verse 2 in our Psalm: "God's gifts come to his beloved ones as they sleep."

We are God's loved ones. Christianity is a love affair. When our personal experience begins to degenerate from being a love affair, the thrill is gone.

71

Christ is the bridegroom, I am the bride. As we enter into a love relationship, something is born from that union.

Our spiritual usefulness is always a result of our love relationship with Christ. In a sense we become spiritual fathers and mothers. Our relationship with Christ brings fruit, brings forth children, new converts, a ministry.

We are responsible for our spiritual children. Have you ever tried to force your beliefs on another? Have you tried to argue someone into the Kingdom? Have you pulled someone into church and pushed them up to the altar to give their hearts to Christ? Three weeks later they are gone.

You say, "Lord, I don't understand why those people did not stay with it." His reply: "Because they haven't been born."

Ministries that are born out of our relationship with Christ produce fruits. Fruitfulness should not be a strain or a struggle. We can hardly wait to share what is born in us as a result of our relationship with the Lord.

I can bring you to Jesus Christ, but I cannot love Him for you. You have to love Him yourself. You have to learn that you are free, that you are His and that He is yours. He wants to love you and let the Spirit of the Lord come upon you, that you may bring forth fruit.

Pray that God will separate the religious

from the spiritual in your mind. When that prayer is answered, it will start a revolution. Because there will be such dramatic changes in your own understanding of what God is doing. God wants a love relationship with us. And through that relationship is born the will, the workings, the gifts, and the ministry of the Holy Spirit in our lives.

What we need most are spiritual fathers and mothers who know how to bring forth fruit in God, so that we may come to understand the Father heart of God and see the ministry of the Lord worked *in* us and *through* us by the Holy Spirit.

Psalm 128

1 Blessed is every one that feareth the Lord, that walketh in his ways.
2 For thou shalt eat the labor of thine hands; happy shalt thou be, and it shall be well with thee.
3 Thy wife shall be as a fruitful vine by the sides of thine house; thy children like olive plants round about thy table.
4 Behold, that thus shall the man be blessed that feareth the Lord.
5 The Lord shall bless thee out of Zion, and thou shalt see the good of Jerusalem all the days of thy life.
6 Yea, thou shalt see thy children's children, and peace upon Israel.

Experiencing Spiritual Maturity

The word blessed—both in Hebrew and in Greek—can be translated, "to be envied." The same word is used in the beatitudes, where it says: "Blessed is he who . . ." It should be translated as: "To be envied is the man who is poor in spirit." "To be envied is everyone who feareth the Lord, that walketh in his ways."

What are God's ways?

Isaiah 55 says: "My ways are not your ways " God's ways are 180 degrees different than our ways. God seldom does things the way we think He should.

Let us pray for your husband, presupposing that he will come to church, go forward and give his heart to Christ. Instead he becomes mean, physically violent, and one night he goes out and gets drunk. He has an automobile accident, and in the ambulance he says: "Dear Jesus, save me."

"Lord," I say, "I wouldn't have done it that way." But God declares: "That is to show you that My ways are not your ways."

When are we going to learn that we cannot

anticipate what God will do? You will always be in confusion until you say: "God, I don't care how You do it, just do it!"

I have watched Him work in the strangest ways.

Once, while home from Bible college, I needed five dollars to get back to campus. I stood in our church and watched all the people I knew who could help me, walk out the door. Finally there was just me and a little old widow lady. I knew she was poorer than a church mouse. I thought, Oh, well, I guess I can walk 110 miles. "Bob," she said, "you wouldn't be offended if I gave you this, would you?" She gave me a five-dollar bill, and I stood there overwhelmed, because she was the least likely person in the whole church for God to use in this way.

We cannot anticipate God's ways.

For ten years I prayed for God to teach me His ways. I even wanted to know the whys, the hows, and the wherefores.

One verse of Psalm 77 tells us that God's ways are in the sea, there is no path. To Joshua He said: "You have never gone this way before; you have no choice but to follow me."

No two healings recorded in the New Testament are alike. One concerned spit and mud; another was, "Go wash in the pool." Another was a laying on of hands, and still another was just speaking a word. Some people think they are going to learn the secrets of divine healing. There is only one secret of divine healing: Jesus.

Earlier in life my idea of an apostle was a big, bombastic, self-assured man of God. One day I read what Paul said: "I came to you with fear and trembling."

The more we know about God, the less we know. One of the wisest men who ever lived said: "I do not know how to go out, and I don't know how to come in."

When we begin to see that God's ways are not our ways, we begin to think differently, talk differently, move and act differently. We have different financial attitudes, different marital attitudes. Something has changed within us.

In verse two the Psalmist says, "For thou shalt eat the labor of thine hands."

This is spiritual productiveness. It is not human labor, but a cooperative venture between God and His children. We are beginning to produce.

We have defined spiritual maturity as that time when you begin to produce more than you consume.

I remember the first prophesy I gave. Even as I spoke I could feel my head swelling. I thought, this church is fortunate to have a prophet. The moment God began to use me I got all puffed up. When we begin to learn His ways we realize that we are doing nothing of ourselves. We are only workers together. God does not do it alone, and we cannot do it alone. We are workers together, not *for* God, but *with* God. There is an important distinction.

In verse 5 we are promised: "The Lord shall bless thee out of Zion, and thou shalt see the good of Jerusalem all the days of thy life."

In order to find God, we must find Him where He is. If you are looking for Him where He is not, then you have problems. The doctrine of omnipresence means that God is everywhere. But God is particularly at certain places and in certain situations where He can be found.

"The Lord shall bless thee out of Zion," as our chapter's Psalmist speaks. Zion is the city of God, where God dwells. For years it was a geographical place—Jerusalem, in Israel. If God is going to bless *me* out of Zion I must know from where those blessings are coming. Many people are looking for God to do something "out there," wherever that is. But God has chosen to dwell in our hearts. That is where we find the city of God. If He is ever going to bless us, we must look for Him in our own hearts.

Jesus came to save us, to cleanse the temple. *We* are called the temple of God. *We* are cleansed so that we can be fit for God to dwell in us.

This is why we must first meet Jesus as the Lamb of God before we meet Him as One who dispenses the promise of the Father.

In Colossians 1:5 we read: "For the *hope* which is laid up for you in heaven, of which ye heard before in the word of the truth of the gospel. . . ."

Our hope is in heaven. Wonderful! But are we going to wait until we get to heaven, or is God trying to get heaven to us? Look at the next verse in Colossians: "Which is come unto you, as it is in all the world and bringeth forth fruit as it does also in you. . . ."

That's the issue: fruit.

We once had a prophecy in our assembly, "The Lord Jehovah doth feel through the leaves of the vines searching for fruit." The vine is the whole system, and we have a lot of church and religion and little fruit. But the objective is fruit!

What fruit is Paul talking about? Look further in Colossians, verses 10, 11, and 12.

"That you might *walk worthy* of the Lord, unto all *pleasing,* being *fruitful* in every good work, and *increasing in the knowledge of God; Strengthened* with all might, according to his glorious power, unto all *patience and long-suffering with joyfulness;* Giving thanks unto the Father, who hath made us *capable* [that's the correct translation of the word 'meet'] to be partakers in the inheritance of the saints in light."

Now to verses 23-27 of Colossians 1: "If ye continue in the faith, grounded and settled, and be not moved away from the *hope* of the gospel, which ye have heard, and which was preached to every creature that is under heaven; whereof I, Paul, am made a minister. Who now rejoice in my sufferings for you, and fill up that which is behind of the afflictions of Christ in my flesh for his body's sake, which is the church, whereof I am made a minister, according to the dispensation of God which is given to me for you, to fulfill the word of God, Even the mystery which hath been hid from ages and from generations, but *now* [I love that word "now" and I have it circled in my Bible] is made manifest to his saints. To whom God would make known what is the riches of the glory of this mystery among the Gentiles, which is *Christ in you, the hope of glory.*"

Paul begins by saying, "I have a hope for you, which is laid up for you in heaven." Where is Jesus? In heaven. This hope is yours if you continue in faith, if you hold fast to the truth of the gospel. Then what will happen? Paul says you will not have to go to the hope. The hope will come to you.

The hope of glory is Christ in you! This has been the mystery that began with the tabernacle. God said: "I am looking for a habitation, a place to dwell, and one day I shall dwell in them."

Paul saw it. May God help the Church to see it! Let us look at 2 Corinthians 6:16.

"And what agreement hath the temple of God with idols? for ye are the temple of the living God; as God hath said, I will dwell [the Greek word means to take up residence or dwelling place] in them, and walk in them . . . and they shall be my people. Wherefore, come out from among them, and be ye separate, saith the Lord, and touch not the unclean thing and I will receive you. And will be a Father unto you and ye shall be my sons and daughters, saith the Lord Almighty."

Having therefore these promises, dearly beloved, let us hold fast to the hope of the gospel, which is Christ in you.

For many years most of us have been taught that God's blessing was going to come some day . . .

The Psalmist now is beginning to come out of all the religious confusion and the talk about getting there "someday." He begins to talk about God dwelling and ruling in Zion. He talks about God-inside-mindedness. That is what you have when you begin to know where God is.

We don't have to understand why God does it this way, or how. All we need to know is that God chose to dwell in us. We must become God-inside-minded.

The Scripture says: "Seek ye first the Kingdom of God and his righteousness." That means that we are to seek for God to establish His rulership over our lives and He will take care of all the other things.

If God cannot establish His Kingdom in you as an individual, then He cannot establish His Kingdom in the earth. Because you are the living stones, His building material.

Psalm 129

1   *Many a time have they afflicted me from my youth, may Israel now say.*

2   *Many a time have they afflicted me from my youth; yet they have not prevailed against me.*

3   *The plowers plowed upon my back; they made long their furrows.*

4   *The Lord is righteous; he hath cut asunder the cords of the wicked.*

5   *Let them all be confounded and turned back that hate Zion.*

6   *Let them be as the grass upon the housetops, which withereth before it groweth up.*

7   *Wherewith the mower filleth not his hand; nor he that bindeth sheaves his bosom.*

8   *Neither do they which go by say, the blessing of the Lord be upon you; we bless you in the name of the Lord.*

Embracing Suffering as the Balancing Factor

It has always seemed strange to me that people think their walk with God is going to be all glory.

The Lord sees to it that you stay in balance.

When there is revelation or special blessing from God it is glorious, and then He sends a little messenger to fall in the other side of the scale.

Picture a man who is progressing in his Christian walk. He is beginning to see God in his circumstances. God has been dealing with him and he is beginning to be God-inside-minded. Now he feels undaunted and says: "Oh, if I just had the devil here I'd rub his hide full of salt." The only trouble is, the devil shows up and he rubs your hide full of salt.

We all go through it. No one likes to suffer, I am not a martyr. But it is part of the package. Paul says in Philippians 1.29, "For unto you it is given in the behalf of Christ, not only to believe on him, but also to suffer for his sake."

Do you know why? Suffering is the balancing factor. When we see somebody receive a special blessing from God and there is no suffering, it is time to be worried.

Paul said: "I saw a revelation . . . and lest I be exhalted, there was a messenger." I personally believe it was a demon. The Greek uses a masculine gender, and I think Paul was tormented by something in the form of a person.

God knows how to set up suffering.

Notice in verses one and two of the Psalm that here is suffering but no distress. If you suffer and don't understand why, then there *is* distress. I say, "God just let me know what's going on and then I will embrace it. But I cannot suffer for nothing."

Once when told to take a saw and cut some trees down, I asked "What for?" I want to know why. If they tell me that they want to cut a fire path or need some kindling wood, or whatever they want the trees for, then I'll cut.

If you understand why you have to suffer you will not revert to your old escape mechanisms.

If you are God-inside-minded you know that Christ in you is the hope of Glory. You know that you are not going to the hope, but the hope is seeking to establish Himself in you. Knowing that, you find yourself going through the necessary suffering without batting an eyelash. In fact, you are singing and rejoicing!

One of the fruits of the Spirit is long-suffering with joyfulness. "For the joy that was set before him, he endured the cross."

In the New Testament church, every time there came a new flood of God's glory, persecution followed. It is the balancing factor. It is always there. When God moves, when He gives you a deeper understanding in Christ, there is a balancing factor.

The Psalmist says: "Many a time have they afflicted me from my youth; yet they have not prevailed against me."

I would like to invite you on a trip to a beautiful country called Vietnam. The foliage is lush and beautiful. There are birds and butterflies, and at night you hear the monkeys chirping. . . . To tell only half the story gets people into confusion. If I am going to take you to Vietnam I must tell you about Viet Cong land mines, the problems and the dangers. Do you still want to go?

When the Israelites came near the Promised Land they sent spies ahead. They came back and told that there were fierce-looking giants in the land. Caleb and Joshua said, "Well, we know they're over there. Hallelujah, God will deliver them into our hands. Let's go!"

I go around telling people there are giants in the Promised Land. But few people want to stay home. Because I came back with grapes. They taste one and say, "I never tasted anything like that; where did you get them?" I reply, "I'll tell

89

you where they grow, in the giant country!"

In the realm of the deeper life there are dangers. Some people crack up. Some are deceived and go off in the wrong direction.

Just because some airplanes crash I don't stay on the ground. People get killed in automobiles, but I still drive.

I know that suffering is the balancing factor in my life and I say, "Thank you Lord for keeping me balanced. You know what I need and I do not."

Every minister experiences the sensation of particular success. On an occasion such as this, I stood at the door and shook hands with the people. A rather distinguished looking man came up to me, shook my hand and said: "That's good preaching—if you like that kind of preaching." He caught me with my guard down, and I was so wounded I wanted to quit. "Lord," I cried, "Why!" The Lord said: "Embrace it, you needed it."

You see, I thought I was doing pretty well. When we are feeling pleased with our own spirituality God says: "It is time to be balanced."

In verse three the Psalmist says: "The plowers plowed upon my back."

This speaks also of the Lord Jesus. Years ago, a Christian had a vision of the Lord being beaten with the cat-o'-nine-tails. He saw the Lord tied to the whipping post. In those days they hung them up so high that their feet could not touch the ground and the Lord's body was painfully stretched. The Roman soldier was flailing at Him and the blood was flowing. In the vision, this person ran up to grab the Roman soldier and as he turned him around he saw his own face. God spoke to him in the vision and said: "For your sins, for your healing was this done, You did it to Him."

You should hear that particular person share the realities of Calvary.

Have you ever had someone run a plow up your back? A church, a dear friend, always someone you know well, because you do not let anybody else near enough to hurt you.

"The plowers plowed upon my back; they made long their furrows."

Some people misinterpret God's outpouring of His Spirit. The early rain comes to get the ground ready for the plow. Before the rain, the ground is too hard for the plow. So the Lord pours out of His Spirit and His blessings upon people and they think that is the end. That is only the beginning.

After the blessings of the Lord rain upon you and you are tender and spiritual He comes along and plows your spirit wide open.

He may do it Himself or permit someone else to do it, but either way you must be opened for the entrance of the seed.

Then comes the healing of the wound, the time of production; first the blade, then the ear, then the full corn. The latter rain comes to mature the harvest. The cycle goes on and on.

When the rain comes, I say: "Thank you, Lord, for the rain. Thank you, Lord, for the plow."

I do not run from the plow any more. I embrace the plow. I need it. You know the song, "Oh cross that liftest up my head, I dare not ask to fly from thee. I lay in dust, life's glory dead, and from the dust there blossoms red, life that shall fuller, richer be."

Verse four: "The Lord is righteous, . . ."

Verse five: "Let them all be confounded [that's the same word as confused] and turn back that hate Zion."

When you begin to move into God you discover that the people you thought would embrace it do not. The children of the flesh persecute the children of the Spirit.

I am not talking about people with a martyr complex. If you are doing things in order to be persecuted, that is your business. There are self-made martyrs who keep everybody stirred up and then wonder why everybody picks on them.

"Happy are ye if you are persecuted for righteousness sake." The joy of the Lord is evidence of maturity.

When you ask some people how they are doing, they say, "Fine, under the circumstances." The response to that should be, "What are you doing under there?"

The mature Christian learns to say "Things are wonderful. The rent isn't paid, the kids are sick, the tires are flat, and everything is wrong. Hallelujah!"

Verse eight: "Neither do they which go by say, the blessing of the Lord be upon you."

Do you expect approval from people? How disappointing to wait for people to say, "We bless you in the name of the Lord," and they don't do it.

Read Isaiah 66:5 "Hear the word of the Lord, ye that tremble at his word: Your brethren that hated you, that cast you out *for my name's sake.*" (They thought they were doing God a favor.)

When God poured out His Holy Spirit and the charismatic movement began to spread through the large denominations, many churches were embarrassed. There were healings and speaking in tongues and other manifestations of the Spirit, and some pastors and church members were asked to leave. God permitted it. They needed that balancing factor.

Look at Acts 8:32-33. These verses have kept me when the giants came and everything went wrong. ". . . He was led as a sheep to the slaughter . . . so opened he not his mouth." And verse 33 in Mumford translation: "While he was under the dealings of God he didn't get a fair deal." That is an accurate translation of, "In his humiliation his judgment was taken away." Did Jesus get a fair deal? Or did they lie against Him? Did they bring false counsel, did His disciples forsake Him? Peter lied and cursed and said he didn't know Him. It seemed as if God Himself had forsaken Him.

While you are under the dealings of God, please do not expect a fair deal. The injustice is part of the package. They will lie against you, testify against you, take you to the court, indescribable situations can happen. Do not say, "How could they do this to me." They didn't. God did.

No parent likes to see his child suffer. He would rather take it himself if it were possible. I dislike punishing my children, but it is necessary. And from it comes the fruit of righteousness.

Honestly, have you run from God? Have you been afraid of His dealings? Have you been afraid to say, "Take all of me, Lord," because He might put you through something you could not stand?

I would not ask from my son something he couldn't produce. How much more, then, does God see to it that we are never faced with more than we can take?

Are you going to embrace the Hope of Glory?

Psalm 130

1 Out of the depths have I cried unto thee,
  O Lord.
2 Lord, hear my voice; let thine ears be attentive to the voice of my supplication.
3 If thou, Lord, shouldest mark iniquities, O
  Lord, who shall stand?
4 But there is forgiveness with thee, that thou
  mayest be feared.
5 I wait for the Lord, my soul doth wait, and in
  his word do I hope.
6 My soul waiteth for the Lord more than they
  that watch for the morning; I say, more
  than they that watch for the morning.
7 Let Israel hope in the Lord; for with the Lord
  there is mercy, and with him is plentous
  redemption.
8 And he shall redeem Israel from all his iniquities.

Revealing Ourselves to Ourselves
(Allow God to reveal us to ourselves)

This is one of the most difficult steps on our journey so far. God reserves this step until we are ready, and now we are coming very close to the core of the human spirit.

We have not said very much about sin. But now we are talking about a believer who has come quite a way out of confusion. He is finding some spiritual maturity, and spiritual usefulness. The tide has been turned, he is beginning to move out to others, and he is becoming God-inside-minded.

There must be a certain degree of spiritual maturity before God can reveal you to yourself. If God did this while you were yet a child in Christ, while you were in confusion, it would be more than you could take.

God comes, by the Holy Ghost, to reveal your self as you really are. To reveal you as you appear in His sight, to unfold and reach down into the depth of your spirit to bring up the things that you are afraid to look at.

This does not happen to many believers, because so few mature enough to embrace it.

97

The Bible says that no man can see God and live. Does this mean a physical death? In searching the Scriptures, I began to see how God deals with His children.

When God revealed Isaiah to Isaiah, the prophet said, "My God, I am a man of unclean lips, I dwell with unclean people."

When God revealed Himself to Ezekiel, he was as "one dead." When God revealed Himself to Daniel, Daniel was as one dead. Even John the beloved, the one who had laid upon His breast, said of himself when the triumphant, resurrected Christ appeared to him, "I fell as one dead."

When God reveals Himself to man, something inside dies. You are never the same again.

Many believers never come far enough out of confusion to enable God to do this for them. Consequently, we see many great ministries shut up in odd personalities.

See the ministry in that man, look at the gifts, what an anointed man! But he has some quirk in his personality, some strange thing he cannot let go of so that God could really use him as He desires to. Haven't you met good ministries in strange vessels? They move on a restricted level because they never come to the place where God can reveal them to themselves.

Robert Burns has said: "Oh would some power the giftie gi'e us, to see ourselves as others see us."

I've said, "Never mind, Lord, I don't need that gift."

Once you really begin to see what God is doing you become frightened. God desires to dwell in us and seeks to open us so that we may be cleansed and ready for Him.

The Psalmist says: "Out of the depths have I cried unto thee." He is under the hand of God. God is beginning to reveal him to himself by the ministry of the Holy Spirit.

While in Bible college we had a prophetic utterance that said: "Examine yourself before the Lord." We fell to our knees and began to pray. After a while another utterance came to declare: "I said examine yourselves, not each other."

We were saying, "This is what they need. This is good for so and so." Have you ever wondered who "they" are in the church? "They" said this, "they" did that, and "they" need to repent.

The Psalmist says: "Lord, hear my voice. Let thine ears be attentive to the voice of my supplication. If thou, Lord, shouldst mark iniquities . . ." That word should be translated lawlessness, which describes an undisciplined human spirit. When we say iniquities, one thinks of adultery or other overt sin, and that is not what we are talking about.

We are talking about the lawless, undisciplined human spirit. That something inside which refuses to submit to the will, purpose, or even the direction of God.

"If thou, Lord, shouldst mark iniquities, O Lord, who shall stand?" Now suddenly the Psalmist is looking at himself. I don't mean introspection. If you are constantly looking inside yourself you will have problems. There comes a time when God Himself, by the Holy Spirit, will turn a searchlight of heaven on the inner man and begin to reveal you to yourself."

There is one prayer that God likes to answer. You find it in Psalm 139, where David cries out: "Search me, O God . . . " If you have never had an answered prayer, try that one. There is always a very fast answer!

"Search me, O God, and know my heart. Try me and see if there be any wicked way . . ." This is when David was coming under the inspection of the Holy Ghost. God was revealing David to David so that David could understand himself.

Most people are afraid to recognize themselves. One personal plague is stubbornness. I have honestly desired to be free from it for some time. The other day while driving down the road, my five-year-old son was in the car. There was a little dog lying dead by the side of the road. My son said, "There's a dead cat." I said, "Son, that was a dog." "It was a cat," he insisted.

"It was a dog," I repeated. He smiled and said, "It was a cat." With all the authority I could muster I said, "Who knows best?" "You do," he replied. And I said, "Daddy says it was a dog." He said, "Yes, Dad."

We rode along for about five minutes, until the air was cleared and Daddy's spirit subdued. Then the boy said, "It could have been a cat!"

God said: "Now Mumford, get a little taste of that, a chip off the old block."

I can tell it now, but there was a time when that was a touchy subject. When someone touches something in your life and you get angry, it is said, "If he gets your goat it only proves you have one." Inside we have many things that God wants to bring out into the open. God will show you either by direct revelation or by putting you in certain circumstances to show you by your reactions what is inside you.

I knew two men who had been close friends for many years. One became involved with his secretary and fell into adultery. His friend became very judgmental and criticized him severely. He spoke religiously of how God was displeased and how God's honor was dragged in the mud. One night the Spirit of the Lord came upon him and in a dream he saw himself standing over a bottomless pit. All was darkness, and the Lord walked up and removed the robe of righteousness from him. He felt himself falling, falling.

101

Suddenly, out of the depths he cried, "O God!" He stopped falling and God said, "What shall I do for thee?" and he said, "Give me back my righteousness." God replied, "Why should I give you righteousness when you have uncovered your brother's nakedness?" He said, "Father, if You'll return to me the righteousness of Christ, I will dispense righteousness and mercy to my brethren." He was returned from the pit, the robe was put back on him, and he woke up.

You should hear him share on grace now!

You don't really know what is inside you until you are placed under the proper pressure. Then you will either find out by direct revelation or God will permit some happenstance to put you under enough pressure that whatever is in you will be revealed.

You think you would never do certain things? Wait until God puts the right pressure on, and you will be amazed to find out what comes out. "Dear Lord, was that in me?"

While in the Navy I made my commitment to Christ. Shortly thereafter, while inspecting the ship's galley, I pulled out a large breadboard. It slipped and crushed my thumb. I exclaimed: "My, oh, my, oh, my." The Navy cook looked at my thumb and at me and asked, "What's happened to you?" Later it dawned on me that God had allowed that situation to show me that there was cleanness in my heart. My language had

102

changed!

We need to say something about deliverance from mixture. Mixture is seldom understood in Christian circles. When listening to ministry we must learn to discern the degrees of mixture. Is this 30 percent man and 70 percent God, or is it 60 percent man and 40 percent God, or 98 percent God and 2 percent man?

If we are ever to come out of confusion, we must understand God's desire to deliver us from mixture. He wants to increase the degree of purity in you so that you can move and minister in a purer vein. Man cannot do this for himself. God must do it for him.

This is why Paul says, "Let the prophets speak, let the others judge; prove all things, hold fast to that which is good." You must learn to discern and understand the content of the mixture. God will purify His Church.

Good ministries are shut up in some odd personalities, with strange ideas and wrong concepts. They cannot come forth until they are mature enough for God to reveal them to themselves.

We once lived in a home overlooking the Atlantic Ocean. I often was up early to watch the sunrise, which I enjoyed greatly. It blessed my soul and I used to minister to the Lord and He would minister to me. I was getting spiritual at last, so I thought.

Then the Lord said to me: "Tomorrow morning I want to minister to you." I said, "Yes, Lord," and was filled with anticipation. I got up early, with my Bible, . . . and waited. Suddenly the Holy Spirit came, and He began to reveal to me what was in me until I was on my face in the rug. The tears flowed, the hand of God was heavy upon me. He began to reveal to me the iniquity and lawlessness in my spirit until finally I cried, "God, stop, lest I die!" The Spirit of the Lord lifted from me. "God, if you mark iniquities, . . . who can stand?" Look at Psalm 19:12. "Who can understand his errors, cleanse thou me from secret faults." The Hebrew translation reads: "Who can tell how oft he offended?" Who can tell how often we offend God?

We think we are walking straight, but we are really comparing ourselves with ourselves. I am not trying to put you in bondage. I am trying to bring you out of it. This is glorious liberty. For unless you grow to the point where God can trust you enough to reveal you to yourself, you will always be shut up in some type of strange personality.

In verse 5 (Psalm 130) the Psalmist says: "I wait for the Lord . . ." You have to wait, because it takes time for you to mature to where God can reveal you to yourself.

I waited, and waited. "Lord, show me if I am

as stubborn as my wife says I am." And out of the mouth of my son comes illumination of my own stubbornness. "Thank you Lord, I see that." We learn to recognize the voice of God in all circumstances.

God does not reveal in order to condemn. God reveals in order to redeem. Blessed is the man who is dealt with by God and the Lord reveals to him his own peculiar personality, his own quirks, his own rebellion. God does not do that to condemn. Satan is the one who presses down in condemnation. God reveals in order to heal and deliver.

Matthew 1:21: "Thou shalt call his name Jesus, for he shall save his people *from* their sins."

Verse seven: "There is mercy and . . . plenteous redemption." Everything God reveals to you is for the purpose of redemption. He does not do it to show you how imperfect you are, but so that you can know what He already knows about you.

Verse eight: "And he shall redeem Israel from all his lawlessness."

We must not retain a lawless spirit. Our lawlessness must be revealed and redeemed. This is a positive step out of confusion.

Psalm 131

1 Lord, my heart is not haughty, nor mine eyes
   lofty, neither do I exercise myself in great
   matters, or in things too high for me.
2 Surely I have behaved and quieted myself, as
   a child that is weaned of his mother; my
   soul is even as a weaned child.
3 Let Israel hope in the Lord from henceforth
   and forever.

Finding Our True Selves
(and Place in the Body of Christ)

Please never get up and say you hate yourself. God loves you.

You must find your true self. If you do not know who you are, how can you come out of confusion?

In verse one the Psalmist declares: "My heart is not haughty, nor mine eyes lofty, neither do I exercise myself in great matters or things too high for me."

For years the church had what we call a "one-man band." An evangelist would come to town with a drum, a clarinet, and a mouth-organ, and he played them all. He would also do the preaching, and the prophesying, and the verse he would use for all this is "I can do all things through Christ."

If that is Paul's intent, then why does God provide different gifts and ministries to make up the Body of Christ?

God is finished with the one-man band. We have come to the day of specialization. We must find our true self and our place in the Body of Christ. This cannot happen until God has revealed you to yourself; then you know what you are.

John the Baptist said: "The mountains shall be brought down and the valleys shall be brought up to make a straight path for the coming of the Lord." There are some who think they are like mountains and cherish exaggerated ideas of themselves. They must come down! On the other hand, there are those who think they are valleys, who despise themselves. They say: "I am so unworthy. There couldn't be a place for me in the church." These 'valleys' must be brought up!

Some people belittle themselves so that God cannot use them, others think they can do everything and confuse the issue. Between them they will find the mountains come down and the valleys come up in order to make a straight path for the coming of the Lord.

Romans 12 teaches us how the mountains are brought down and the valleys are brought up.

Paul declares: "For I say through the grace given unto me to every man that is among you, not to think of himself more highly than he ought to think, but to think soberly, according as God hath dealt to every man the measure of faith . . ." The J.B. Phillips translation reads, "Don't cherish exaggerated ideas of yourself."

If you cherish exaggerated ideas of yourself

you will always be in confusion. If you think God called you to win the world all by yourself you had better read this verse again.

Everyone has a place and a calling. Everyone, no matter who you are.

That is thinking soberly. Every man has a gift ministry, a portion of faith that God has given him. You are responsible for it. Begin to find your true self and your place in God. You are not a valley nor a mountain!

In verse two the Psalmist says: "Surely I have behaved and quieted myself . . ."

Do you think behavior is important? Look at 1 Samuel 18:9-15.

"And Saul eyed David from that day and forward . . . And Saul was afraid of David because the Lord was with him and was departed from Saul . . . Therefore Saul removed him from him and made him his captain over a thousand, and he went out and came in before the people. And David behaved himself wisely in all his ways, and the Lord was with him. Wherefore when Saul saw that he behaved himself very wisely, he was afraid of him."

There have been many with mighty anointings, but they did not understand the necessity of behaving themselves.

The devil is not afraid of you because you are anointed by the Holy Spirit. The only time he is afraid is when you are anointed *and* know how to behave yourself.

If Saul had seen over-confidence or rebellion in David, he would have said, "I'll just wait a little while and he'll destroy himself." But when he saw that David behaved himself his reaction was one of jealous resentment.

In 1 Timothy 3, Paul states, "These things write I unto thee . . . that thou mayest know how thou oughtest to behave thyself in the house of God." Some Christians need to learn how to behave!

For three years as a Pentecostal in an Episcopal Seminary, I was on the Dean's list, I obeyed every rule, I handed in every lesson. In every way, I walked circumspectly before those men. I behaved myself as I realized actions are as important as words. It was here that I learned to appreciate and love these men of God. Our fellowship expands and confusion ceases when we learn to behave.

The Psalmist goes on to say in verse two: ". . . as a child that is weaned of his mother; my soul is even as a weaned child."

Most people fuss when the Lord begins the weaning process. In America we wean babies early, take them off the bottle and put them on strained baby-food. But in other countries

112

children nurse at the breast until they are three, four or five years old. And when it comes time to wean there is some powerful reaction.

People say: "Oh, I want the fire by night and the cloud by day." A cloud by day and a fire by night was for the rebellious Israelites in the desert. When they finally were weaned from the cloud and the fire they moved into the land where the manna ceased.

If you want to hear loud crying, wait until the spiritual manna ceases. The initial experiences of childhood must, at some point, cease.

Many who live on past experience are continually seeking to regain past blessing. Because of change they feel they have sinned or "lost their first love."

When you are young in Christ you are as a baby in diapers. You are enjoying the good things of the Lord, and then one day God comes to remove the diapers. You stand there naked, unable to pray or read. The Bible reads like the *New York Times.* Christians do not understand. Their advice is to pray more and read more, but you cannot. Spiritually stripped we cry: "Dear Lord, give me my long pants!"

While we are growing between diapers and long pants we stand spiritually naked. We reach back for diapers so many times. "God, I don't know if I want to go on, I just want my own diapers back. Permit me to sit and sing in the

113

crib and have a wonderful time."

Then one day the Father appears, slips a pair of pants on you . . . and they are knickers! "Thank you, Lord, for the knickers."

One day the knickers come off and you stand naked again. During growing stages there are times when you stand spiritually naked. Finally you get a pair of gray pin-stripe trousers. You are embracing the Fatherhood of God, approaching unto maturity where you may father others in the Spirit.

God has brought you through!

God wants you to find yourself, and your place in Him. And when you do, His joy and satisfaction will fill you. I do not want to be like someone else. I want to be me. God is revealing the real me.

Psalm 132

1 Lord, remember David and all his afflictions;

2 How he swore unto the Lord and vowed unto the mighty God of Jacob;

3 Surely I will not come into the tabernacle of my house, nor go up into my bed;

4 I will not give sleep to mine eyes or slumber to mine eyelids.

5 Until I find out a place for the Lord, an habitation for the mighty God of Jacob.

6 Lo, we heard of it at Ephratah; we found it in the fields of the wood.

7 We will go into his tabernacles; we will worship at his footstool.

8 Arise, O Lord, into thy rest, thou and the ark of thy strength.

9 Let thy priests be clothed with righteousness, and let thy saints shout for joy.

10 For thy servant David's sake turn not away the face of thine anointed.

11 The Lord hath sworn in truth unto David; he will not turn from it; Of the fruit of thy body will I set upon thy throne.

12 If thy children will keep my covenant and
   my testimony that I shall teach them,
   their children shall also sit upon thy
   throne for evermore.

13 For the Lord hath chosen Zion; he hath desired it for his habitation.

14 This is my rest forever; here will I dwell: for I
   have desired it.

15 I will abundantly bless her provision; I will
   satisfy her poor with bread.

16 I will also clothe her priests with salvation:
   and her saints shall shout for joy.

17 There will I make the horn of David to bud; I
   have ordained a lamp for mine anointed.

18 His enemies will I clothe with shame, but
   upon himself shall his crown flourish.

Union with the Lord

David is looking for a house for the Lord. And he says, "I will not come into the tabernacle of my house, nor go up into my bed; I will not give sleep to mine eyes nor slumber to mine eyelids until I find out a place for the Lord."

The cry of David's heart was not how many mansions *he* would get one day. As long as that is a goal you will always be confused. We are looking for the house where God dwells. David says, "I want to know, I won't sleep until I find a habitation for Jehovah."

David wanted to build a house for God, but God said, "No, you cannot build me a house, I will build *you* one."

We have suggested that the place where God wanted to dwell from Genesis 3 onward is in the hearts of His people. This is where He has desired to live and this is where He is building His temple.

David wanted to know the habitation of God. So should we.

The prophet Ezekiel declares (11:16): "Therefore say, Thus saith the Lord God; although I

117

have cast them far off among the heathen, and although I have scattered them among the countries, yet will I be to them as a little sanctuary . . ." We are little sanctuaries, we have a little Holy place inside.

Early in the morning the song service begins. Quiet follows, for prayer time comes next. And if you will cultivate your sensitivity, the ministry of the Word will follow.

New Testament Christianity is a mystical union. I am God-inside-minded. I do not look for God out there; I know where He is.

God sent Jesus as the Lamb of God for the cleansing of the temple. Jesus saved me, and I am cleansed in order to receive the promise of the Father. It is the Father who desires to come and dwell in us in the power of His Holy Spirit. That is why He sent the Son. For thousands of years since the entrance of sin, God was shut up in a Tabernacle or Temple. At last when His Son was nailed to the tree, the Lamb of God was slain, sin was atoned for. The Bible says: "The earth shook and the stones broke and the veil in the temple was rent." God had torn it from top to bottom not only that we may have access, but also that He might openly have fellowship with His people.

Jesus ascended, the Holy Ghost descended, and this is the promise of the Father. He said, "I will dwell in them and walk in them." That is the great mystery of the ages.

David says in verse eight, "Arise, O Lord, into thy rest, thou and the ark of thy strength." The ark contains the bread and the laws and the life. There is Aaron's budding rod. In that small ark was all the truth and power that God had given His people.

Look at verse 13: "For the Lord hath chosen Zion, He hath desired it for His habitation."

I don't understand why God desires to dwell in Zion. But He chose it. He chose it for His own purposes in the earth. In the beginning of time He walked with Adam and Eve, and the Bible says they knew Him and there was communion between them. Sin cut that off. When God came looking for Adam and Eve they were hiding.

God has been looking for a people ever since the entrance of sin spoiled His first community. Do you still wonder why God wants to deal with you? His desire is to free you from your bondage of loneliness, your selfishness, your erroneous concepts. God is seeking a house where He can dwell in liberty.

When I began to understand, I said, "All right, Lord, clean house. Purify this temple. Is it selfishness, criticism, is it strange ideas? Is it money, things, people? Clean it up, because I cannot give rest to my eyes until I find a house for the Almighty."

We talked earlier about our being built together as a house for God, as the New Jerusalem. In Ephesians 2, Paul speaks of how God breaks down the walls between us, between Jew and Gentile, to make one new man That is the man God desires to dwell in.

In verse 18 Paul says: "For through him [Christ] we both have access by one Spirit unto the Father." Not only do we have access unto the Father, the Father has access to us. It is not a one-way street. I know a Brother who prays, "Father, help Yourself to us." That is a legitimate prayer. Lord, help Yourself to us, we are Your people.

Paul goes on to say: "Now therefore ye are no more strangers and foreigners, but fellow citizens with the saints, and of the household of God. And are built upon the foundation of the apostles and prophets, Jesus Christ himself being the chief corner stone. In whom all the building fitly framed together groweth unto a holy temple in the Lord. In whom ye also are builded together for an habitation of God through the Spirit."

We are not talking about the union between individuals. We are talking about the union with God. That's what it is all about. Your access to God and His access to you. God-inside-mindedness.

When you look for guidance from God, look within. Do not listen for strange voices out there, listen for guidance from within. He chose to dwell in you, and He said, "Out of your belly or inner being shall flow rivers of living water."

The Psalmist speaks of God's provisions:

"I will satisfy her poor with bread. I will also clothe her priests with salvation [that means everybody], and her saints shall shout aloud for joy. I will make the horn of David to bud [that is authority] and I will give her a lamp [that is light or truth]. His enemies will I clothe with shame, but upon himself shall his crown flourish."

The man who comes into union with God becomes indomitable. He is stable in God. He knows his God and God knows him.

Psalm 133

1   Behold how good and how pleasant it is for
    brethren to dwell together in unity.
2   It is like the precious ointment upon the
    head, that ran down upon the beard, even
    Aaron's beard; that went down to the
    skirts of his garments.
3   As the dew of Hermon, and as the dew that
    descended upon the mountains of Zion;
    for there the Lord commanded the blessing,
    even life for evermore.

Union with our Brethren

For brethren to dwell together in unity is not only good and pleasant, it is also miraculous and infrequent.

The greatest miracle of Pentecost was that they were all in one place with one accord. I heard a theoretical explanation of how this happened. They were gathered together, Mary, Peter, Bartholomew, James, John and Phillip and 114 other disciples, to wait on the Lord. They waited and waited until finally the human spirit began to settle. God made them wait for ten days. About the sixth day Mary got up and said, "You know, even though He was my own Son I did not always believe Him." Peter got up and said, "Of all failures, I am chief." James stood to say, "Remember in the garden, when we all forsook Him?" One by one they got up to confess their faults until finally they were reduced to nothing. The result was called "one accord."

The only time we can ever be in one accord with our brethren is when we are reduced to nothing.

What a glorious thing it is when brethren get together in unity. How did Jesus say that men will know we are His disciples? By the gifts of the Spirit? By our preaching?

"If you have love one for another . . ."

Love is the only things that cannot be counterfeited. You can counterfeit lesser things, but not the supreme gift. The supernatural love of God—*agape*—defies imitation. You can pretend until something happens to reveal what is really in you. The mask of hypocrisy wears through quickly. Only the man who walks with Jesus knows an unending supply of love, for himself, and for others.

Union with God is one thing. Union with your brethren is another. The cross is both vertical and horizontal. Your union with God is not complete if it does not embrace your brethren. It is easy enough to fellowship alone with God, but oh, the rest of God's family!

The spiritual secret is this: *when we come into union with our brethren the blessings flow automatically.*

God said: "*There* (where brethren are in union) will I command a blessing." It must come because we are on receiving ground.

Some attempt to twist God's arm. "Please, God, we need an outpouring of Your Spirit. Loosen up, God, You know our sincerity, fasting, and prayers."

When you beg for God's blessings and they do not come, it is not because He doesn't want to give. If He gave you what you asked for under those circumstances, God would have taught you the wrong concepts.

To receive the blessings of God in full measure we are required to come into a relationship with our other brethren, with the Body of Christ.

Our own bodies have many bones, but many bones do not make a Body. In the valley of dry bones lay a whole pile of bones.

Ezekiel began to prophesy: "Dry bones, hear the word of the Lord." And they began to come together, and you can be sure it was a noisy meeting.

Isolated bones cannot do anything. Only when they come together can they function as a unit: "To whom coming as unto a living stone, disallowed indeed of men, but chosen of God, and precious, ye also, as lively stones are built up a spiritual house, an holy priesthood, to offer up spiritual sacrifices, acceptable to God by Jesus Christ" (1 Peter 2:4, 5).

We were once out in the world as sinners. We came to the Living Stone, He saved us, filled us with His Holy Spirit and we have *become* living stones.

How tragic that there are so many "hermit Christians" in the world today. Saved, but walking out of step with the Body of Christ. Living stones who refuse to be cemented into place. Yet we cannot know *full anointing* until we are built together.

The first step is to come to the Living Stone. Secondly, you become a living stone. Third step, you are built into a spiritual house. If you do not permit yourself to be welded into the household of faith, you will be cut off from a rich vein of blessing and power.

Anybody can be spiritual all alone. There is no one to challenge you. If you are so spiritually poverty-stricken that no one loves you enough to challenge and correct you, then you are in trouble. I welcome the correction of my brethren, for it is part of the process of being built together.

We know a measure of anointing because we have been filled with the Holy Spirit and have become the dwelling place of God, but we can never know the full measure of anointing until we are built together into a spiritual house where the Glory of God can dwell.

I have been in meetings where there has been a great degree of unity. The presence of the Lord comes in such a way as to evidence God's approval. When we are built together in unity the presence of God comes. It is not necessary to pray for it; it is yours.

"The Lord commanded Life for evermore," says the Psalmist. I do not think that is in the future. I think it is now. If I am in union with

God and in union with my brethren, the anointing will come flowing over the whole priesthood. That means us: "That ye might be a holy priesthood," declares Peter, for the purpose of ministering to others.

In the last few years God has been teaching us what life is all about. Life is getting the house prepared so that He who is Life can take up His habitation. He begins to relate you to other stones and builds you up together. One day the glory of God begins to fill that building, and when it does, the sudden realization of *what* has happened cleanses us from confusion.

Psalm 134

1   Behold, bless ye the Lord, all ye servants
     of the Lord, which by night stand in the
     house of the Lord.
2   Lift up your hands in the sanctuary, and bless
     the Lord.
3   The Lord that made heaven and earth bless
     thee out of Zion.

Bless the Lord!

Twice in this Psalm we are told to bless the Lord. Once the Psalmist says the Lord blesses us. That is producing more than you can consume. Most people are never interested in blessing the Lord, they only want the Lord to bless them. Here the direction has been changed inside.

The fifteenth and last step on our journey is to bless the Lord.

We have come into Zion and we are standing in the temple, the house of the Lord.

"Bless ye the Lord all ye servants which by night stand in the house of the Lord."

What does it mean, standing by night?

Let's go to Revelation 22:11. "He that is unjust let him be unjust still, and he that is filthy let him be filthy still, and he that is righteous let him be righteous still, and he that is holy, let him be holy still." This is not a very accurate translation. The Greek verbs are in the present progressive tense and it is interesting to read the verse that way: "He that is unjust let him be more and more unjust. He that is filthy, let him

become more and more filthy. He that is righteous, let him become more and more righteous,
he that is holy let him become more and more
holy."

There are two visitations, presently, in the
earth. There is not only a maturing of the
Church, but also a maturing of sinners.

The line is being drawn right down through
the Church. That which is holy is becoming
more and more holy. The abounding of sin and
iniquity is forcing us into God. Isaiah 60:1-2
says: "Arise, shine, for thy light is come and the
glory of the Lord is risen upon thee. For behold
the darkness shall cover the earth and gross
darkness the people. . . ."

It is important to realize that in God's program, He seldom changes the circumstances.
He changes the believer.

For years I prayed: "Dear God, change that
man, he is an offense." God hasn't changed him
yet. But He has changed something inside me
and I have finally learned to live above that
thing that upset me.

If you are going to come out of confusion into
God it is not what happens outside of you that
counts. It is what happens inside. There is darkness all around, and inside you are saying:
"Bless the Lord, O my soul."

The riots, the stock market, the war and the
news. But God is inside. I am related to God and

to my brethren. There is night all around, but there is light inside.

There may be darkness in your own church, but there is light in you. Though you dwell in the midst of most upsetting circumstances, though the boat is full of water and the waves are breaking and they say, "Master, don't you care that we perish?" He replies, "Oh, ye of little faith."

Look at Psalm 110 and underline the last part of verse 2. Make it your very own: ". . . Rule thou, in the midst of thine enemies."

God wants to establish His Kingdom within you so that you can rule in the midst of your enemies.

God may not change your enemy, He is going to change you; so that you can stand by night in the sanctuary and lift up your eyes and bless Him.

The only person who can do that is one who has been delivered from confusion.

We began by quoting three questions from Habakkuk: *"How long* shall I cry and you do not hear?"* The second one: *"Why* do you show me iniquity and cause me to behold grievance?" The third: ". . . *Wherefore* lookest thou upon them that deal treacherously, and holdest thy tongue when the wicked devoureth the man that is more righteous than he?"

In chapter 2, verse 1, Habakkuk says: "I will

stand upon my watch and set me upon the tower, and will watch to see what He will say unto me and what I shall answer when I am reproved."

Habakkuk is saying to God, "I want some answers and I want them tonight." God says: "You are in confusion, prophet, and there need be some changes made."

In chapter 3:16, Habakkuk describes how God dealt with him: "When I heard, my belly trembled, my lips quivered at the voice, rottenness entered into my bones, and I trembled in myself, that I might rest in the day of trouble, when he cometh up unto the people, he will invade them with his troops."

At last we find the prophet, standing by night in the sanctuary, blessing God:

"Although the fig tree shall not blossom, neither shall fruit be in the vines; the labor of the olive shall fail, and the fields shall yield no meat; the flock shall be cut off from the fold and there shall be no herd in the stall; Yet will I rejoice in the Lord, I will joy in the God of my salvation. The Lord God is my strength, and He will make my feet like hinds' feet, and He will make me walk upon mine high places."

What had God done? He did not change his circumstances. Everything happened *within* the prophet. When we are seated with Christ in heavenly places, confusion is not possible, for we see things from His perspective.

If the fruit trees do not blossom, if there is no cow in the stall, and if the fields refuse to yield, I'll say, "Hallelujah, Praise His Name!"

God will not change this world for you. He will change you in this world. He can produce a spirituality in you that is undaunted. His pleasure is to teach you how to rule in the midst of your enemies. When there is night all around there is light within you, and you stand in the sanctuary blessing the Lord.